Praise for
Something Beyond Greatness

"An absolutely amazing book! A transcendent blending/integrating of science and faith yields an inspiring awareness of our power to create greatness through supernal service."

—**Stephen R. Covey**, author of *The 7 Habits of Highly Effective People* and *The 8th Habit: From Effectiveness to Greatness*

"Dedicated to those who serve the world, *Something Beyond Greatness* is a science and spirituality classic. My favorite section, featuring 'A Man of Science and a Woman of God,' creates a wonderful reversal: science becomes a home for the soul, and spirituality gives us the fresh and heightened ability to observe. And both are mutually enriched in their focus on the ways and powers of love. When we see the world with a spiritual literacy, and when we take to heart the biologist's life-centric focus on how the best in life inspires the continual creation of what is best in life, we frequently find ourselves moved to wider and wider circles of service. This precious volume is a special guide and path to this combined concept, a more unified understanding, of real greatness."

—**David Cooperrider**, creator of Appreciative Inquiry Professor and Chair of the Center for Business as an Agent of World Benefit Case Western Reserve University

"Judy Rodgers's and Gayatri Naraine's reflections and thoughtful dialogues with cognitive biologist Humberto Maturana and revered spiritual master Dadi Janki clearly articulate the big step that we need to take if we care about each other and the world we inhabit together. They poignantly reveal to us that our individual and collective 'greatness' depends upon the degree to which we are willing to take that heroic leap beyond everything that we have known, making the all-important room for the miraculous powers of the original creative impulse or God to work through us, as us. In a time when we all know how much our world needs to change quickly, this inspiring message can't be heard enough!"

—**Andrew Cohen**, spiritual teacher and
founder of EnlightenNext

"What is it that makes someone turn their life over to humanity? It can be a life's journey or it can happen in a second. I know from my own experience of holding a loving vision for Patrick Sonnier as he died in the electric chair, that what other people see as our greatness often doesn't feel like greatness to us. It feels like the only thing we could do in that moment. This fascinating book describes the powerful urge that turns a regular life into a great life."

—**Sister Helen Prejean**, Roman Catholic nun who wrote the
story of her own life and work in the book *Dead Man Walking*,
which was subsequently made into an award-winning film

SOMETHING BEYOND GREATNESS

SOMETHING BEYOND GREATNESS

*Conversations with a Man of Science
and a Woman of God*

Judy Rodgers and Gayatri Naraine

Health Communications, Inc.
Deerfield Beach, Florida

www.hcibooks.com

The authors would gratefully like to acknowledge the publishers and individuals who granted us permission to reprint the cited material (including biographical information).

Hafsat Abiola, interview with authors, Kent, England, March 2006. Reprinted by permission.

"A Man Down, a Train Arriving, and a Stranger Makes a Choice," by Cara Buckley, *New York Times*, January 3, 2007, A1. Reprinted by permission. ©2007 *The New York Times*.

Father Pierre Ceyrac, interview with authors, Paris, March 2006. Reprinted by permission.

"What Good are Positive Emotions?" by Barbara L. Fredrickson, *Review of General Psychology* 2, no. 3 (1998): 300–19. Reprinted by permission of Barbara L. Fredrickson.

(Continued on page 111)

Library of Congress Cataloging-in-Publication Data
Rodgers, Judy.
　　Something beyond greatness / Judy Rodgers & Gayatri Naraine.
　　　　p. cm.
　　ISBN-13: 978-0-7573-0781-2 (trade paper)
　　ISBN-10: 0-7573-0781-7 (trade paper)
　　1. Altruism.　2. Helping behavior.　3. Conduct of life.
　　I. Naraine, Gayatri.　II. Title.
　　BJ1474.R63 2009
　　177'.7—dc20

　　　　　　　　　　　　　　　　　　　　　　　　　　　　　　　　2009002917

Publisher: Health Communications, Inc.
　　　　　　3201 S.W. 15th Street
　　　　　　Deerfield Beach, FL 33442–8190

Cover design by Jean Brennan
Interior design and formatting by Lawna Patterson Oldfield

To
Dadi Janki

CONTENTS

FOREWORD

Great leaders are first and foremost great human beings.

Greatness is all around us and has many faces. Every day, everywhere, we see and experience people living lives of service and caring for others.

We see heroic actions of people risking their own lives to save others; we see people suffering to alleviate the suffering of others; we see people giving up their social lives to create life for others; we see people dedicating their whole livelihood to create livelihood for others.

I have come to believe that all human beings possess these innate qualities to give love, to care, to grow, and to create a sense of belonging for others. Equally, I have come to believe that all human beings have an innate need for love, care, growth, and to belong. But for these innate qualities to manifest in a congruent and consistent way seems to require a certain character of the beholder and a particular context that evokes them.

Why is it that some human beings are able to develop their characters in such a manner that greatness is not only manifested in an incidental "act," but becomes a way of life?

Why is it that human beings of riches and human beings of poverty can both decide to live a whole life of service and care for others?

Why is it that some human beings are able to extend their circle of influence in a manner that affects the whole world?

Some people will explain these elevated human beings as being instruments of God. Others will refer to evolution and the "biology of love." Still others will emphasize the influence of context and early childhood experiences.

We obviously do not know why some human beings are living a consistent life of greatness. But regardless of whether we understand the phenomenon or not, we all seem to recognize when a great person is in our midst. We feel it, sense it, and see it! There is a quality of "being," a quality of love that resonates with all of our innate needs for love and peacefulness, of unconditional acceptance of who we are.

I have always been interested in what is involved in the journey to being a great human being and a great leader.

While we might not be able to explain why some people live lives of greatness, we do know that we can help leaders to "experience and see" moments of greatness and bring them into contact physically and spiritually with those who are gifted with greatness. When we bring leaders into contact with greatness, we give them a chance to develop the right intentions of service and the right attitudes of abundance, compassion, and humility. Face-to-face experience with greatness also helps them to develop a kind of wisdom that they need to become more effective in their endeavors. It's wisdom in harmony with the right intentions of service and care that turn people into great human beings. It's great human beings who become great leaders and help this world to become a better place for all of us.

—*Tex Gunning,*
AkzoNobel managing director,
Decorative Paints

CHAPTER ONE

THE INSPIRATION

I n 2006, Dadi Janki, renowned spiritual leader in India and a dear friend, turned ninety. As one of the leaders of the Brahma Kumaris World Spiritual University, she has been traveling widely, speaking at conferences, and sharing spiritual wisdom with thousands of people on all continents for many decades. Because she is a friend to so many around the world, there were birthday celebrations in many places— on stages in London, in tents in Oxford, in halls in India, and everywhere in between. In early 2004, anticipating this auspicious occasion, two of us proposed that we would like to create a book in her honor—a book on greatness. She listened politely and then declined, saying she had no interest in a book in her honor. Undaunted, we proposed a book dedicated to what she has given her life to—a book dedicated to those who serve the world. She considered the idea and gave her consent.

We shared the idea with our friend, Tex Gunning, who offered to support the book project. Tex, who is managing director at the Dutch company AkzoNobel, is a passionate lecturer, writer, and speaker about the role of business in society and about the need for collective leadership to tackle the world's biggest challenges.

We decided to begin with a search for those who have dedicated their lives to world service. We thought about what it is that makes Dadi Janki so unusual in the world—so inspiring to so many. From this churning, we created a list of criteria that described what we were looking for.

We ran the list of criteria by Tex; Peter Senge, MIT lecturer and author of *The Fifth Discipline*; and Humberto Maturana, a friend and world-renowned biologist who specializes in the biology of cognition. We polished the list and refined it a bit and prepared to begin a formal search for candidates with "something beyond greatness." The result looked like this:

A Search for Those with "Something Beyond Greatness"

CRITERIA

At this fragile time in the world, there are many who are moved to make a difference. However, there are certain special souls who are called to go beyond making a difference and who surrender their lives to humanity, touching all of those they meet. We are undertaking a search to try to understand the quality of character that defines these "world servers," people like Indian political and spiritual leader Mahatma Gandhi, and Mother Teresa, who won the Nobel Peace Prize in 1979 for her work with the poorest of the poor in India. What is it that causes them to live the inspiring lives that they do?

We believe these people can be found on all continents, on all religious paths, and in different generations. However, regardless of the differences, we believe they share certain qualities. We are seeking to find and interview people who appear to have the following qualities or characteristics:

- A quality of mind that is characterized by those who know him or her as stable, peaceful, and compassionate.

- His/her service is dedicated to improving the life and/or awareness of others with no self-interest.

- He/she explains their work in the world as coming from a higher power or source: they understand themselves to be an instrument and have the quality of humility that comes from that understanding.

- Their own life is characterized by the same principles they stand for in the world: their inner life and their outer life are completely integrated.

- They seem to others to be tireless, drawing on a deep well of energy that appears to give them endless endurance and unlimited patience.

- They have an elevated vision of those they serve, seeing their capacity for renewal, recovery, and progress so clearly that those they serve find strength they didn't know they had.

- Their convictions about what they are doing are so strong that they are unfazed by limitations in funds or support from others.

- They have a quality of lightness in their life and work and are surprisingly available in the moment—even though they are heavily scheduled and have immense responsibility.

What is most interesting about those who have this ineffable quality we are referring to as "beyond greatness" is that while each has done important and transformative work in his or her life, it is the quality of their being that seems to do the most service. People describe being transformed simply by being in the presence of those who have this character of "beyond greatness."

It is this way of being, as well as the moments of understanding and growth, that has allowed them to arrive at this quality of character that we aspire to convey in a book.

Next, we gathered a group of thinking partners, friends on all continents, who had greatness in them and who certainly knew people who they would consider great. We sent them this list of criteria, requesting they send names of people who would meet these criteria. We found someone who would help us with the sorting and vetting of the volume of names we anticipated, and then we waited. And waited. Finally, we heard from a couple of the thinking partners. One wrote from Australia to say, "I have given a lot of thought to your request and to these criteria, and I just don't know anybody like this. If you find somebody, though, let me know. I would love to meet them." Then we heard from the thinking partner in Brazil, "Can they be dead?" Since we intended for the book to be based on interviews, we declined to include dead people, hoping to find "greatness" alive in the world. Person by person, the responses came in—pretty much echoing the first two.

We called Tex and requested a meeting in New York. A few weeks later we were sitting together in the Meditation Center and Gallery of the Brahma Kumaris on Fifth Avenue, laying out the dilemma. We explained that there was virtually total unanimity on the names of certain historic figures, such as Mother Teresa, Mahatma Gandhi, and Martin Luther King Jr. But when it came to finding this same quality of character in the living, people seem stumped—really having no idea who to suggest. We were feeling discouraged. Tex listened closely and then pronounced the situation to be promising. We were perplexed. What, we wondered, about this stalled project was he finding promising?

Carefully, he explained, "The fact that everyone agreed on a few names suggests that we know greatness when we see it, which must mean that we have greatness—or the possibility for greatness—in us. Greatness must be intrinsic in each one. We just have to discover more about this." He urged us to push ahead, saying it didn't matter how many people we profiled. It was more about the quality of what we found. So we persisted.

CHAPTER TWO

THE SEARCH

E ventually, names did start to come in. Our researcher sent us batches of material. What we found was that many people—thousands and maybe hundreds of thousands of people—have dedicated their lives to helping others, starting nongovernmental organizations (NGOs) and creating foundations for everything from helping children to curing Alzheimer's. They were all good people. But were they great people? As we began to assess their lives and work against our criteria, we found it hard to give a resounding "yes." It was more like a tempered "well, maybe."

We decided that the best approach was to select a small number of people from those who had been recommended to us—a diverse sampling of continents, ethnicities, and gender. We would start by interviewing them. Maybe when we were sitting with them and hearing their stories, we would feel the greatness we were searching for. So that is what we did.

We sat with Abdul Kalam, then president of India, at the presidential palace in Delhi; with Federico Mayor, former director general of UNESCO and architect of the Culture of Peace initiative at a university in Madrid. We met with Hafsat Abiola from Nigeria when she was in Kent, England. Abiola had lost her parents in political assassinations and subsequently started a nongovernmental organization to train women leaders. We flew to Scotland to meet with the principal of a teacher education establishment and educational thought leader, Bart McGettrick, and to Paris to meet with Father Pierre Ceyrac, a Jesuit priest who had dedicated his life to helping orphans in India. Our friend and colleague Christina Carvalho Pinto interviewed Zilda Arns Neumann in São Paolo, Brazil.

Each time, we turned on our tape recorder and began to inquire with them into this growing mystery called "something beyond greatness": "What is it the world most needs at this time?" we asked. "What is it that makes someone turn their life over to service of humanity?" "Was there an experience that moved you to make this kind of choice about your own life?" "We would like to understand what goes on inside of your mind and heart relative to the service that you do," and so on.

Because they really are wonderful people, each one tried in earnest to answer our questions, listening closely and then offering their own stories, struggles, and victories. None of them claimed to be great. In fact, all of them cited others who they thought were great. One of them went so far as to tell us, as we were leaving the interview, "Now, don't use my name in this. I am not a great one."

By the end of the interviews, we were no closer to understanding "something beyond greatness" or to understanding the inner workings of true world servers than we were when we started. Humbled and pensive, we went back to the drawing board. We decided that what we needed was to reflect on greatness further, perhaps using the stories we had garnered in these interviews as a basis for reflection. We agreed on two people who we would most like to have as thinking partners on the subject of greatness. We checked in with Tex again, this time with a different proposal: *Something Beyond Greatness: Conversations with a Man of Science and a Woman of God.* "Go for it," he said. So we headed to Chile.

A MAN OF SCIENCE

We had known Humberto Maturana and his wife, Beatriz, for many years. In fact, a number of years prior, he and Dadi Janki had been together as the science and spiritual resource people in a dialogue in Chile. They had gotten along very well, and their different perspectives on life and truth had proven very complementary. We asked Maturana if he could clear some time to meet with us, and he obliged. Maturana is first and foremost a reflective man, an original thinker, and a compassionate friend. He is a professor of biology at the University of Chile in Santiago and founder and director of the Laboratory for Experimental Epistemology and the Biology of Cognition. Maturana has achieved international renown as a neurobiologist and is a leading exponent of modern systems thinking. He is the author of several books, including the international bestseller *The Tree of Knowledge*, written with his disciple, Francisco Varela.

One subject on which he has written and spoken widely is "The Biology of Love." He believes that in the subject of greatness, as in the subject of life itself, understanding comes back to the subject of love: "Love occurs when one behaves in a way such that those around you arise as 'legitimate others' in coexistence with you. In our daily life we say that we feel loved when we are in a relation, in which there are no expectations or demands placed upon us, so that we do not have to justify our presence. Love does not expect retribution. The other can appear as he or she is, without pretending to be what he or she is not. Love is a biological, relational disposition and does not need philosophical or religious justification for being there."

A key to Maturana's understanding of love is that it does not place expectations or demands on others. In working with Maturana, to understand his notion of greatness, this was a recurring theme. He said, "When I speak of greatness, I speak of a behavior that encompasses wisdom, understanding, and detachment in a domain of human relations."

To set a context for his reflections, we asked him, "What is a scientist?" He responded thoughtfully, "What makes scientists, scientists is the disposition to search for understanding or explanation." In this case, the understanding we were looking for had to do with the nature and source of greatness. Maturana helped us to think about the people we were meeting in our search and what it is that made them behave in ways that others characterized as great. With him, it always comes back to love: "Love is a fundamental feature of our biology. A person who one might be willing to say is 'beyond greatness' is someone who is open to letting others be— someone who is able to listen and see and let the other be, in such a way that his actions do not constitute a demand for him to deny his history or the natural flow of his living."

He offered an example: "There is a nun who has this place where she collects children. She is supported by the church, because she is a nun of this church. She offers the children the possibility to be themselves and does not demand anything of them, but provides a culture in which their own history can be preserved and where they can grow into self-respecting adults. She doesn't do this as a way to grow the orphanage or for the purpose of indoctrination. I don't remember the name of the nun, but I remember that when she was asked if she attempted to convert the children to Roman Catholicism, she answered, 'No, they have their own histories and beliefs. I just give them love.'"

For Maturana, love—real love—has to do with the very act of seeing the other as a legitimate being: "To see, you must let the other be and not put your expectations or purpose on them. Because if you put expectations on them and your expectations are not satisfied, you are disappointed. Then you will not see the other. All you will see is your unmet expectations. When I see with the attitude of 'let it be,' without my expectations or desires, then seeing and loving are the same thing. You don't really see if you don't love. To love is to let it be."

A WOMAN OF GOD

Of course, our love and respect for Dadi Janki had been the genesis of the book project. Dadi Janki is the chief of the Brahma Kumaris World Spiritual University, an international nongovernmental organization headquartered in Mount Abu, Rajasthan, India. As a spiritual movement and learning community, the Brahma Kumaris emphasize the inculcation of universal principles taught by God to humanity for spiritual renewal of the individual and the world. While she holds the title of administrative head of an organization of almost one million members in 120 countries, her primary focus is on bringing spiritual wisdom to the world. Early in her life, she spent fourteen years in a small spiritual community, using her own life as a laboratory to explore spiritual concepts. At the end of that time, she and the others with whom she lived moved into the world, devoting themselves to applying these concepts in the world. She continuously teaches about the knowledge base of Raja Yoga (a spiritual practice through which one reclaims the natural sovereignty of the self through remembrance, which we will discuss more thoroughly in Chapter 10) and speaks to huge audiences on spiritual matters. She refuses to be a guru, but is a spiritual friend to many around the world.

She is a person of God and has been since childhood. Her relationship with God is her most important relationship.

She speaks about God as if He is in the next room. He is her father, her mother, her teacher, her guide, and her companion. Though she has been honored and celebrated in many places over the years, and addresses hundreds and thousands of people at a time, she uses these occasions to help people understand what she believes to be the universal truths of life and the importance of the thoughts they think and the actions they take in the world. She takes no credit for her remarkable intellect, but insists she is simply sharing what she has learned from God.

Like Maturana, Dadi Janki also finds love to be the foundation of greatness: "Real love doesn't deceive nor does it allow itself to be deceived. Where there is selfishness, there is no love. We need to understand what real love is. When there is the experience of God's love, that removes all sorrow. Human love today is often connected with attachment. Someone gives a little love, and the other becomes crazy about them. I don't want love that is going to give me happiness only sometimes. True love gives peace and happiness and makes the heart feel constantly full. So we need to ask our hearts, 'Do I experience true and honest love? Do I have that type of love within?' With true love there won't be any wrong actions performed, because the intellect that is filled with love guides the soul in the direction of truth."

Humberto Maturana and Dadi Janki, Chile, 2002

Humberto Maturana, Dadi Janki and Sister Jayanti Kirpalani

CHAPTER THREE

A MAN OF SCIENCE AND A WOMAN OF GOD

What Humberto Maturana and Dadi Janki share is an interest in the explanations of what is most fundamental in life and a respect for the experience and questions of others. They both believe in the importance of the choices one makes to act in a certain way. And they both work from a basic understanding that the feelings of love that one has for oneself and for others are the ground from which life-affirming action proceeds. They also share a belief that human beings are intrinsically loving. It is our nature.

However, there is much on which they differ. While they both explain life, the scientist, Maturana, "attempts to explain 'the doings' he sees in the living of life." The spiritual person, Dadi Janki, attempts to explain the quality of character of the being who is acting in the world. Maturana believes that the foundation of character begins in the loving and caring—or the lack of a loving and caring—environment in which the being grows up, often the home and the relationship a child has with her parents. Dadi Janki believes that the foundation of character resides inherently in the soul, that the qualities and virtues that manifest in our thoughts, feelings, relationships, and the actions we take in the world create the environment in which we live.

Humberto Maturana and Dadi Janki also differ on the question of where the possibility for transformation or improvement of the human being lies. Maturana says, "This particular biologist believes the possibility for this is only in the coexistence with other human beings." Dadi Janki believes that the only hope for real transformation of the human being is in our relationship, our coexistence, with God. In asking them to reflect with us on something beyond greatness, we were hopeful that they would help us get to the ground truth about what distinguishes those we call great.

Expanding the Search for Greatness

As we pored over stories of those deemed to be great and interviewed people about their experiences with greatness, we focused on specific accounts, stories of moments in which people extended themselves with remarkable courage, generosity, or compassion. What we quickly realized is that the quality of greatness we were looking for was not the exclusive province of those recognized publicly for their greatness.

Abdul Kalam, then president of India, gently emphasized this point in our very first interview. He said, "The question is, who are you? If you ask me, everybody here is a unique person. Everybody is not a big personality like the great ones. Every human being writes a small page in history; every human being—irrespective of how big or how small—writes a small page. That is real human history. Real human history is not just 15, 20, or 30 great leaders for whom we are searching. The whole human history is a record of every human being who is born in this universe, on this planet. That's the idea, isn't it? Because I believe human history cannot be said to be a history of great human beings—the history of a few people."

He did concede that although everyone is unique, some have a greater impact in the world. He and his friend Arun Tiwari talk about this in a book they coauthored on "guiding souls" (*Guiding Souls: Dialogues on the Purpose of Life*

[Ocean Books, 2005]). Kalam says, "So in our book both of us were asking, 'who are the guiding souls?' In our searching we found a whole spectrum of people who are guiding souls. A small consultant can become a guiding soul."

Eventually we expanded our search beyond those who had been recommended to us and began to include the invisible actors who, in living their otherwise ordinary lives, engaged in acts that others would deem great. We peered into each story as if we were looking through a microscope into a petri dish, examining each story for clues about greatness.

In these beautiful stories, we began to make out the contours of an emerging pattern. It had three elements: (1) seeing with love, (2) acting from the heart, and (3) the mystery of destiny—right place, right time. Each story appeared to begin with the "hero actor" seeing the other with a vision of love. Maturana refers to it as seeing the other as a "legitimate other." Dadi Janki refers to it as seeing with "soul-conscious" vision. He or she sees the other with a sense of belonging, as one might look on a brother or sister. The actions they took emerged from this loving vision. Sometimes they acted in an instant. Other times they weighed their actions carefully, but always they acted from the heart and not from the head. When something comes from the heart, it is as if a mysterious and unlimited capacity becomes available to the actor, and all of the questions of the head—such as who, what, and how—fall away. What we found was that when these two aspects—seeing with love and acting from the heart—aligned with the right moment in time, it was as if an invisible door opened and the hero actors moved swiftly through it, stepping into some kind of a subtle current of destiny, in which things happened that they never could have planned. Even time seemed to cooperate in these emerging miracles. This pattern repeated in story after story of greatness.

CHAPTER FOUR

MOMENTS OF GREATNESS

One story that captured the public imagination was the story of the man who in 2007 became known as the "subway hero" in New York. Here is the story, as told by Cara Buckley of the *New York Times*, on January 3, 2007:

> Who has ridden along New York's 656 miles of subway lines and not wondered: "What if I fell to the tracks as a train came in? What would I do?"
>
> And who has not thought: "What if someone else fell? Would I jump to the rescue?"

Wesley Autrey, a 50-year-old construction worker and Navy veteran, faced both those questions in a flashing instant yesterday, and got his answers almost as quickly.

Mr. Autrey was waiting for the downtown local at 137th Street and Broadway in Manhattan around 12:45 PM. He was taking his two daughters, Syshe, 4, and Shuqui, 6, home before work.

Nearby, a man collapsed, his body convulsing. Mr. Autrey and two women rushed to help, he said. The man, Cameron Hollopeter, 20, managed to get up, but then stumbled to the platform edge and fell to the tracks, between the two rails.

The headlights of the No. 1 train appeared. "I had to make a split decision," Mr. Autrey said.

So he made one, and leapt.

Mr. Autrey lay on Mr. Hollopeter, his heart pounding, pressing him down in a space roughly a foot deep. The train's brakes screeched, but it could not stop in time.

Five cars rolled overhead before the train stopped, the cars passing inches from his head, smudging his blue knit cap with grease. Mr. Autrey heard onlookers' screams. "We're O.K. down here," he yelled, "but I've got two daughters up there. Let them know their father's O.K." He heard cries of wonder, and applause.

Power was cut, and workers got them out. Mr. Hollopeter, a student at the New York Film Academy, was taken to St. Luke's Roosevelt Hospital Center. He had only bumps and bruises, said his grandfather, Jeff Friedman. The police said it appeared that Mr. Hollopeter had suffered a seizure.

Mr. Autrey refused medical help, because, he said, nothing was wrong. He did visit Mr. Hollopeter in the hospital before heading to his night shift. "I don't feel like I did something spectacular; I just saw someone who needed help," Mr. Autrey said. "I did what I felt was right."

Wesley Autrey acted in a split second. He saw Cameron Hollopeter was in jeopardy and leaped onto the tracks in front of an oncoming train. Whatever he saw in that moment when Cameron fell onto the tracks evoked an instant response in him. Maturana and Dadi Janki would likely call it love. He acted from that loving vision and in an instant joined the ranks of those heroes who stand as persistent evidence of a fundamental goodness within everyday people.

For many, the case of Wesley Autrey brought to mind similar acts of courage on another January morning twenty-five years earlier—the crash of an Air Florida plane into the icy Potomac River in Washington, D.C. Maturana recalled it spontaneously during our conversations in Chile: "There was, in Washington, D.C. many years ago, a very big snowstorm, and an airplane was leaving and accumulating snow on its wings so fast that it fell into the river. It fell into the river and got entangled in a bridge and people began to drown. There was a man who stood on the plane's wing, helping people to get out. Others called 'You come now.' But he said, 'No, there are still people here to be helped.' And he was carried away. When the helicopter came, he was gone. What would someone say about this person? That he was great, but about what was happening in his mind, we have no idea."

Some people have speculated on what might've been going through this man's mind that particular day, but we will never really know for certain. What we do know is that he exemplified aspects of greatness by sacrificing himself so that others might be saved.

Articles about this historic crash appeared as we were working on the manuscript for this book. The story of the twenty-fifth anniversary of this famous crash was published in the *Washington Post*:

> That day—January 13, 1982—was a tragic one in the Washington area. As a blinding snowstorm gripped the region, Air Florida Flight 90 clipped the 14th Street bridge on takeoff and plunged into the river, killing 74 passengers and four people on the bridge.
>
> Amid the chaos and sadness, several acts of bravery stood out: a helicopter pilot who plucked survivors from

the freezing river; a medic who climbed out to grab a victim too weak to help herself; two bystanders who could no longer bear to watch helplessly from the sidelines. One of the injured passengers, later identified as Arland Williams Jr. of Atlanta, drowned after passing the lifeline repeatedly to others.

The *Post* recounted the stories of some of the other heroes who took action that day, so we do have some idea of what was going on for them:

Roger Olian looks back on what he did and chuckles. Then a sheet-metal foreman at St. Elizabeth's Hospital, he was the first to try to reach the few survivors clinging to part of the plane's tail section in the twenty-nine-degree water. As other people on the riverbank held one end of a makeshift rope fashioned of battery cables, scarves and pantyhose, Olian took the other end and set out toward the screams. Rescue workers had not yet arrived.

"I was stupid," said Olian, now 60, of Arlington. "I had all these keys in my pocket. I had five pounds of keys. I didn't even think to take them out."

He did not think at all before acting, he said. He just knew he could not stand idly on the shore watching people drown or freeze to death.

Lenny Skutnik, a federal employee on his way home from work, swam out to rescue a drowning stranger. Images of his heroic acts stuck in the public imagination.

"I remember when we first got down to the riverbank, there was no rescue equipment. It was very quiet—that eerie quiet when it snows," Skutnik recalled this week. "And out of the quiet, this woman was yelling for help: 'Will somebody please help?'"

There is a sense of inevitability in the experiences recounted by these heroes. It doesn't appear that they felt they were making a choice to act. As Lenny Skutnik said, "What else could I do?" Many of them acted so quickly that there was no time to think—and yet even without thinking they were successful in their attempts to help the other.

Far from wanting to be thanked or recognized for their actions, the "heroes" often express gratitude that they had the opportunity to help. Wesley Autrey said it eloquently, when at the end of his press conference on the day after his heroic save of Cameron Hollopeter, he was asked to reflect on the experience: "What a better way to start the new year than to save a life?"

These stories of greatness—of Wesley Autrey and the men who leaped to action when the Air Florida flight hit the

Fourteenth Street bridge—reveal a kind of inner readiness that seems to appear from nowhere, surprising even those who take the action. However, there are other moments of greatness that we uncovered as we interviewed some of those who had been recommended to us—more considered moments of greatness, acts that were the result of a commitment made after deep reflection that had much of the same character as the sudden acts of greatness.

The youngest person we interviewed was Hafsat Abiola, who was thirty when we met with her in Kent, England. Her story is strongly tied to the story of her parents and the pro-democracy movement in Nigeria. In 1993, Abiola's father, Moshood Abiola, won Nigeria's first democratic presidential election in ten years. The election was subsequently annulled by the ruling military council, and he was incarcerated. He died on the eve of his release in 1998. Abiola's mother, Kudirat, who mobilized pro-democracy groups during her husband's imprisonment, was assassinated in the streets of Lagos in 1996. Abiola shared the story with us:

> The day that my mom was killed, we got a phone call from someone saying that something had happened to her. But we believed her to be so strong, bigger than life, that we never considered that she might be dead. A little while later we got another phone call, this time saying that she had been shot point blank in the head on the

road and was dead. We children stood together holding hands. In that moment I decided I wanted to do something in her memory, something that would carry on what she stood for.

My mom left, with seven children still at home. I was twenty and I was the oldest girl. My older brother was twenty-one. The youngest was nine. I mean, it was very difficult for all of the children. My brother and I were just about to get our first jobs, but I was very glad that she didn't wait for us so she could live her life. She lived her life.

It's this whole idea that a woman must live her life. We need to generate that permission within ourselves, not even so much from society but from within ourselves, that we have a right to aspire to our own dreams, to work for changes in our society, not just within our own family. I feel that that is one of the things I can celebrate about my mom. She was very much involved in scripting how our family was going to be, and then she was also very much involved with scripting how the larger society was going to be. And I wanted other women to draw their inspiration from her for doing that. The problem was that, because of the way she died—because she was gunned down on the road—I felt that if we were not careful, what should be a life to be celebrated would become a life that is a lesson in what not to do, you know, because of the very brutal, violent nature of the way she came to her end . . . because that's what was happening all over Nigeria. People were saying, "But you see, we told her not to do this." And other women would think, "Given what has happened, let me keep my very quiet space. Let me simply take care of my children." So one of the things I did was to create KIND, the Kudirat Initiative for Nigerian Democracy, which is dedicated to promoting democracy and strengthening civil society in Africa.

This year we are training 1,250 young women in five universities around Nigeria, and we want to do that every year for the next five years, and we have a leadership manual that we want to make available to other leadership organizations for free so they can empower women. We're involved in a campaign to get 30 percent of the government positions in the next election. We have a book that was written about her called Kudirat: Steps in Time. When we were fighting for democracy, we had a radio station called Radio Free Nigeria, and when she was killed, the democracy movement chose to rename it Radio Kudirat Nigeria, so they've named the voice of freedom and the expressions of our freedom after her. So many things we have done, all in the memory of this woman. So what could have been a negative lesson, now I am making an effort to turn it into a positive lesson. All of us are going to die. If you don't dedicate yourself to larger issues, then you won't be remembered in this way. Kudirat died in this way, but not all women—or men—will be remembered in the way that she is remembered.

What we felt as we listened to Hafsat Abiola in that living room in Kent was not only the love of a daughter for her remarkable mother, but also her enormous desire for her mother's courageous life not to become invisible, not to be deemed a mistake—"We told her not to do this." She feels the world desperately needs the full contribution of women in "scripting how the larger society is going to be" and created KIND to support women in stepping into those bigger roles. Another child might have shrunk from public view in fear or fled Nigeria. But Abiola's defiant response was to memorialize Kudirat's life in an institution dedicated to being a midwife for bringing women from the quiet confines of domestic life into the public eye of national leadership. She saw her mother's life with compassion and pride and took steps to make sure others could witness this extraordinary life and make their own lives extraordinary as well.

Abiola began a crusade to support the movement of young girls onto the national stage of leadership. But no leader begins on a national stage. Early acts of leadership begin with decisions made in the privacy of a single life. This is what we found in the story of Bart McGettrick, a gifted educator in Scotland. When we asked McGettrick to think back over his career and to share with us a time that he would characterize as a high point, he recalled that all of the significant times involved people. Greatness is based on people and relationships. He especially recalled a time when he helped a young woman facing difficult circumstances to steer her way through pressures and confusion toward making a decision she could live with in dignity:

> I think the high point was to help two or three students who were struggling personally and domestically, which was clearly affecting their academic performance, and to give them a harbor for rest and to see them flourish after that. In particular, I remember one girl who was having difficulties at home. She was expecting a baby. She wasn't married. At the time there was a tremendous pressure from her family to marry and to have the baby in the context of a marriage. She thought she had to leave the college where I was principal. I said to her (a) "Don't marry"; (b) "Don't leave the college"; and (c) "We'll do what we can do to take care of the baby."

With the support of McGettrick, who was the college principal at the time, she took the time she needed. A year and a half later, she married. Eventually she came back and continued her program at the college. She became a teacher. McGettrick saw her more than a decade later when her son was about twelve or thirteen and was about to enter secondary school.

Many of those who perform acts of greatness such as this don't have the benefit of seeing the results of their actions. McGettrick had the added confirmation of knowing that the actions he took on behalf of the young mother and her unborn child played out well in the end. He said:

> It just seemed to me, to be able to hold out one's hand to someone like that in difficult circumstances, where the system would have done something different . . . What I found as a principal is that what gives you the greatest satisfaction is to do something that the system wouldn't do. In the great sweep of life, that may appear to be a ripple on the pond, but in the end, it is what matters.

We asked him if he felt this gesture was an act of love. Again, he said:

> These matters are very much to do with a kind of a professional love, a care you have to have for people. It would not be too strong a term to use. It was an act of love, professional love for a young person. I think this is

something to do with knowing that the pain of the other and the pain of the self are not different. To remember this, to feel this, is simply to be human.

McGettrick mused on the special circumstances of those who are in positions of authority:

> Those who were the keepers of the regulations were a bit put out that here was the one who was the writer of the regulations, and one who was supposed to enforce the regulations, appearing to go against them. I believe that sometimes one's got to review these regulations and the impact they have on young people. I spoke to the people who were objecting to the decisions I had taken. I think one just asks them, what is a good decision? What is right? And you just have to face up to that. That does take a certain amount of personal courage. That means taking the risk and making decisions knowing the consequences. Certainly one's got to watch. It's not courageous just to flaunt regulations. You have to do it with a soul very much in mind. It is not a generalizable thing. There is an important distinction to be made between professional courage and stupidity. The important thing is to do the right thing by an individual.

The story of Bart McGettrick follows the familiar pattern we saw in the stories of "instant heroism"—seeing the other with love, acting from the heart, and the "destiny piece"— being in the right place at the right time.

We asked Humberto Maturana for his perspective on McGettrick's story. What did he see that he would consider to be great? What we came to appreciate with Maturana is that he observed the particular actions of the hero actors within the flow of the circumstances of their lives, noting how their actions opened up possibilities for others to live lives of dignity and self-respect: "I would say that this was an act of love, because this was an act of seeing. What did he see? He saw a girl. He saw the family. He saw the context for living. He saw what would happen to the child in the configuration of events, and he did what was required. He took all of the arrangements into conscious or unconscious consideration, and he acted in a way that gave to this young woman suffi-cient autonomy to live a life that she would consider desirable and respectful. He said, 'Do not marry.' In other words, do not give in to the demands. Eventually she married, but pre-sumably not giving in to the demands of others, but because she thought the moment was appropriate. In this case the principal gave her the possibility; he did something that is very rarely done and that is remarkable. He said, 'We shall do whatever is necessary to help you to bring up the child.' This is an interesting thing, because this is very rarely said. This means I, the college community, will do whatever seems opportune and necessary for this child to grow in a legitimate family circumstance. This is the beauty of this story—that this man took responsibility, because he saw the legitimacy of everything that was in front of him. That is an act of love. That is an act of seeing the other and acting according to what he sees—in the domain of respect—letting the girl arise in her legitimacy without having to apologize."

We then turned to Dadi Janki for her perspective. Generally when we asked Dadi Janki to reflect with us on a situation, she would begin by taking a few moments of silence to reflect from a space of pure thoughts and elevated feelings. And this was exactly what she observed in the story of Bart McGettrick and this student—the importance of pausing and turning within:

"When we are in a difficult situation, we may feel we are under compulsion to make a decision, because of the pressure of time and because of pressure from those involved in the situation. But if we make decisions under pressure, things will not go right. In this case, the one who acted as her professional counselor showed true spiritual insight.

"He would have counseled her to go within, to get in touch with the self and to discover her true feelings about the situation. We must always connect from the inner being to the external situation. Because of the principal's experience, he was able to help her in the right way, taking everything into consideration. If he had overlooked even one aspect in the situation, it would not have worked. It was successful, because no piece was left out. Because of his experience and because of his position, he was able to quiet the atmosphere around the situation, to help her to remove her feeling of panic and to quietly consider the consequences.

"When the atmosphere in which she was thinking had become quiet, she was able to cross over the web of thoughts in her mind. The mind creates puzzles and doubts, but when we cross that and go into the self, we find the way forward is very clear, and we are able to find the truth. It may be that this was a very good life lesson for her—how to listen to her true being while being respectful to the child and the family. If she works on this inner level in the future, she will experience that she has better power to discern and not feel guilty about her decisions. So the quiet heroism of this principal may have shown her something that changed her life beyond that particular moment of choice."

The kinds of actions taken by Bart McGettrick, Hafsat Abiola, Wesley Autrey, and the heroes in the Air Florida crash are taking place continually in colleges, living rooms, and subway stations all over the world, some visible and most invisible. Poetic acts such as these change the course of life in the world, the flow of history. These stories describe moments in which certain remarkable people found themselves sharing a space in time with another who was in need. Instead of seeing the other as a stranger, in that moment they saw them with love, feeling touched with a sense that *in some way this one belongs to me.* This feeling of belonging kindled something in their hearts, and they naturally moved to action, often without giving it a second thought. They acted not from the head, but from the heart, changing their lives and the lives of others through those acts.

In mulling these stories over, it is impossible to unlock the mystery of the chance encounter or the feeling of love that comes over the hero actor. They simply feel that they were in the right place at the right time: the moment appeared, they had the opportunity to be of service to another, and they took it. In their heart of hearts they believe they only did what anyone would have done. Far from congratulating themselves for what they have done, they seem a bit bewildered by the attention and humbled by what happened.

Some men and women lead lives that are an almost continuous flow of such poetic acts. About these people we say not just that they did a great thing, but that they lived a great life—that they themselves were great. It is not so much the quality of the action that distinguishes moments of greatness from lives of greatness. There are remarkable similarities in what we hear from those who have had a single moment of what we might call "greatness" and those who have lived lives characterized as great. For those who have lived lives of greatness, there is a continuity that arises from a flow of benevolent actions throughout their lives.

CHAPTER FIVE

LIVES OF GREATNESS

W hen we began our search for greatness, we found broad agreement on the greatness of certain highly regarded people such as Martin Luther King Jr., Mahatma Gandhi, and Mother Teresa. Of course, we can no longer sit with these great ones to ask them how they saw the situation they were in, what made them choose to act as they did, and how they felt about the role of destiny in their lives. But because they are so famous, some of this insight is available in their autobiographies and in the biographies written by others.

Our research into the life of Martin Luther King Jr. confirmed much of what we had found in those we had studied for moments of greatness. King's determination to help shape a different world is evident throughout his autobiography (published posthumously in 1998 and coauthored by Clayborne Carson). As just one example, King attended Booker T. Washington High School in Atlanta, Georgia (the first black public school, named after another great shaper of history), which was located in a different part of town from where he lived. Because this was during a time when segregation still existed, blacks had to stand in the back of the bus—even if every seat in the front of the bus was empty. King said, "... those seats were still reserved for whites only, so Negroes had to stand over empty seats. I would end up having to go to the back of that bus with my body, but every time I got on that bus, I left my mind up on the front seat. And I said to myself, 'One of these days, I'm going to put my body up there where my mind is.'"

However, years later—after the civil rights movement of the 1960s had reached a momentum and power in the United States no one would have dreamed possible—he talked, not about the determination of his youth, but about being moved along his life path by something greater than himself. He said, "I do remember moments that I have been awakened; ... times that I have been carried out of myself by something greater than myself and to that something I gave myself." Though he knew his responsibility during his time in history, he showed remarkable humility, saying, "I want you to know that if M. L. King had never been born, this movement would have taken place. I just happened to be here. You know there comes a time when time itself is ready for change. That time has come in Montgomery, and I had nothing to do with it."

King's observation that time itself was ready for a change, and that he had nothing to do with it, gives us a glimpse of the mystery behind acts and lives of greatness. We saw similar expressions of humility repeated in story after story. Dadi Janki helped us to see the significance of humility in true greatness: "Each one has a certain part to play in the world, which is why we should never force anyone to do anything. The soul who is in touch with the deepest part of himself will know what he must do. He may feel that he is listening to the call of the time, the call of humanity, or the call of God. When he accepts with dignity that this is the role he has been given to play, then he acts with great humility. Because he is responding to this calling with pure intention, it attracts others to the task on which he is working."

One of the biggest stories of greatness in the twentieth century was played out between two great leaders who also heard the call of their time—one with positional power and one with personal power. The saga of F. W. de Klerk and Nelson Mandela is a story of forgiveness and personal courage.

Federico Mayor, former director general of UNESCO, had a front-row seat for many of the dramas on the world stage from 1987 to 1999. When he met with us, he shared a story about meetings he had with Nelson Mandela and F. W. de Klerk in 1992:

> There is a mystery about human beings; it's this capacity we have to invent and to do what is really against realism, against pragmatism. One such example is what has happened in South Africa. I visited South Africa many times when there was apartheid. As you know, people of color were excluded only because of their skin. In actuality, they should have been the masters in their land. One man, called Nelson Mandela, was in prison. I went to see him in prison, because one of the missions of UNESCO is to support the movements of liberation that are supported by the United Nations. Nelson Mandela was a prisoner for twenty-seven years. Normally, what happens to a prisoner in these conditions? He says with vengeance and hatred, "You will see the day in which I will leave, if I leave, you will see what I will do." But Mandela was thinking exactly the opposite. He was thinking, "The problem is that when I leave here, I must embrace them, and I must say that even though I have been twenty-seven years in prison, I love everybody, whatever they are, blacks or whites." In this case there was someone else who was

playing a critical role in the story of South Africa. You see, we need the other; we cannot do this alone. Mandela found Frederik de Klerk. Frederik de Klerk was such a person. I gave them the first Prize of Peace of UNESCO in the year '92, perhaps '93. In preparation for giving them this award, I went to meet both of them. Nelson I knew before, but when I had a meeting alone with Frederik de Klerk, I told him, "Mr. President, you know that very probably, if you follow this way of friendship with Nelson Mandela, perhaps in six months you will not be president anymore: you will lose all power." And he looked at me and said, "Oh, Mr. Mayor, but at this moment I will be able to sleep very well, because it's a problem of conscience." This was Frederik de Klerk.

Almost everyone alive in the world at the end of the twentieth century felt the touch of greatness in this moment in history. In many ways, the role of Frederik de Klerk was relatively small compared to the spotlight that fell on Nelson Mandela as the first black South African president in the world's newest democratic experiment. But the friendship between Nelson Mandela and Frederik de Klerk, occurring in this particular place and time, and de Klerk's courageous act of ending apartheid sparked a miracle in the history of the world.

Again we turned to Maturana to reflect with us about greatness in this extraordinary moment in the twentieth century:

"This story shows that something acquires significance and meaning only in the flow of events. Because if Mr. de Klerk had thought differently, when the things were happening that created the possibility for the change to take place, he would not have allowed for those changes to take place. Then we all would have said, 'He lost the opportunity. He did not have the vision.' Now, as it turns out, he did not lose the opportunity. He had the vision. This reveals to us what kind of person de Klerk was.

"Meaning is not in the [isolated] action. It is in the history of the flow of events. Meaning is relational. It is not a property. It is not a feature of things. The meaning of an [action] is in the flow of relations . . . in the coordination of doing things in which [the action] participates. So it was very fortunate that it was this particular white man there.

"I think that particular individuals matter always, because it is them—women and men—who are making history, and who are making the flow of events. Some people say that ideas in history exist—that they are 'in the air' and that somehow you pick them up. I do not think this way. I think it is human beings who make things happen, who matter. So in this flow of transformations that we call history, nothing is previous to its happening. It arises in the moment that the human being makes it happen. It is not a development of something that was already contained. It is an emerging. It is a happening of something that is appearing in that moment—something occurring from where it was not. These are poetic acts that are taking place continuously— some more visible, some more marvelous, and some negative poetic acts. It depends on how we live."

Another twentieth-century hero actor who is less well known is Father Pierre Ceyrac, a Jesuit priest who made a choice as a young man to live a life of service to the poor. When we met him at age ninety-three, he had spent more than seventy years serving orphans and street children in India. We interviewed Father Ceyrac in Paris on Ash Wednesday. As he sat down at the table, he removed his watch and put it in front of us all on the table, explaining that at 5:00 PM he would begin a week of silence, something he did each year beginning on Ash Wednesday. We would need to be finished by 4:50. We turned on the recorder and asked him about his life and his work:

> Yes, first my effort is with the children. I've got so many. We went up to 31,000. That was too much for us to cope with. Now we have cut down enormously to 10,000. Between 5,000 and 10,000. We don't try anything. We just love them and admire them. When children sit for a meal, we put a plantain leaf with food in front of

them. We discovered that the children did not touch their food until the last one was served—it can be [a] quarter of an hour. They all sit like this [*he folds his arms across his chest, showing how the children wait for everyone to be served*]. It smells very good—rice with curry. It is delicious when you are hungry. The children are like that. Then they bless their food—that we learned from Gandhiji. Whenever you eat, you bless your food with the children. So we love. The children need to be loved, that's all. And they need education. All of our children are schooled.

Today, but one hour ago, I got a phone call from a girl named Shivane. She is twenty-one now, in the third year at one of the best engineering colleges. We are very happy. So, education, but also with a tremendous amount of love. They have never been loved before, the children we have. They are either orphans—they have no father or mother— or they are street children. We learn from the children.

We don't use the word "organization." It is a movement of children. We would like all the children of India to learn, to love one another, to develop, to grow. We call it a movement of children. If we could get 50,000 or 100,000 one day, we would be tremendously happy. We have problems of course, everybody has problems.

Father Ceyrac is a giant—even among giants. He has worked with Mother Teresa. He knew Gandhi. But you wouldn't know it from talking to him. He is self-effacing and easily moved to tears. All he has done, he says, is to make the poor, the destitute, and the sick feel cared for. According to him, "more than doing something for them, what is important is to make them feel wanted and cared for."

The French government conferred on him the Chevalier de la Légion d'Honneur for a lifetime dedicated to the cause of the poor and the deprived. According to Claude Blanchemaison, the French ambassador to India, the decision to honor Father Ceyrac was taken at the initiative of French president Jacques Chirac.

At 4:45, he picked up his watch from the table, thanking us and reminding us that it was almost time for his silence to begin. "We should work together," he said, "for the spiritual dimension of the world. If not, we go to a catastrophe." He rose carefully from his chair and, with the help of a walking stick, made his way toward the door. As he opened the door, he turned to us and said, "Don't use my name. I am not a great one. Those others we talked about—Gandhi and Mother Teresa—they are great ones." And then he headed down the street toward silence.

These stories of greatness—both those who led remarkable lives and those who stepped forward in moments of greatness, hold the same DNA: seeing with a loving vision, acting from the heart, and intersecting the path of destiny in a heroic way—right place, right time.

We discovered another element in this pattern of greatness: the trademark signs of humility that Dadi Janki said indicated true greatness. In the Air Florida story, the helicopter pilot who pulled four people from the river, Don Usher, insisted, "It wasn't me, it was the helicopter." Wesley Autrey wrote off his heroic act to "right place, right time." When Martin Luther King Jr. reflected on the civil rights movement in Montgomery, he brushed aside the idea that he had led this movement—or even given it a decisive push: "I just happened to be here. You know there comes a time when time itself is ready for change." With Father Ceyrac, his final comment delivered after we had turned off the recorder was the same humble message, "I am not a great one . . . they are great ones."

The expressions of humility were so common in the stories of greatness that we began to consider the possibility that perhaps these men and women really didn't experience themselves as the creators of the acts of greatness. Perhaps what we were hearing from them was the expression of their experience of being an instrument for something bigger than themselves and not the creators of the actions.

CHAPTER SIX

INSTRUMENT
CONSCIOUSNESS

To understand what it means to be an instrument for a higher force, we turned to Dadi Janki:

"God acts through others to accomplish things in the world. And those who carry out the actions are called instruments. In the moment of action, the hero actor does not have the conscious thought of being an instrument, but feels inspired and then compelled to act in a certain way. Only later, when asked about their heroic actions, do these heroes become aware of a certain detachment from the sense of the 'I,' who took these actions. With the feeling of being an instrument, you automatically have the stage of humility. Why? Because your experience is that the act is being accomplished by something bigger than yourself.

"You do not feel that 'I,' this particular personality, has done anything. This feeling of "I" is actually an obstacle to greatness. When you experience being an instrument for God or a higher source, you feel exhilaration—almost intoxication—in the moment and a sense of freedom. I call this feeling 'liberation in life.' It is as if we are acting beyond the limitations of the body."

Instrument consciousness is a phenomenon of the physical world—the world of subway accidents and societies plagued by apartheid. But it is linked to the divine, to inspiration. The person who is about to become a hero actor, in the moment of seeing, is transformed. Awareness is touched, elevated, and transformed. As Dadi Janki says, "They see with love and receive clear, subtle guidance about what they must do. They feel compelled, and they act."

For some, this is an isolated moment in their lives. For others, it is the beginning of a life of such moments—each one utterly unique. Dadi continues, "It is as if they have quietly surrendered inside to this higher force that is touching them and allow[ed] their every step to be guided by this touching. This is why we must continuously live with an openness to these touchings and signals from a higher source."

Dadi's explanation of what it means to be an instrument

confirmed our instinct about the greatness of these world servers. Their humility was the key that unlocked the explanation of their greatness. They didn't claim to have done anything great, because they honestly didn't feel they were responsible for the actions they performed. When asked—or even when complimented—they instantly passed on the credit to someone else, to the helicopter, to the true great ones, or even to destiny itself.

Somehow, in an instant, their life path had intersected with that of someone who needed help. As they looked at the other—in an icy river, on a subway platform, or on the streets of India—they felt love for that one and acted from that love without a thought of anything else. They didn't think about the icy water, the five pounds of keys in their pockets, or the expense of the venture. They simply stepped forward and participated in a miracle. Later, on the other side of the experience, they felt an extreme happiness or bliss. They denied that they had done anything and felt grateful for the gift of this destiny that allowed them to serve in this way.

Armed with Dadi's explanation of what it means to be an instrument, we decided to explore each of the steps of the inner pattern of greatness more carefully, starting with the act of seeing with love.

When we take a closer look at the experience of greatness as revealed in story after story of these hero actors, we see the very subtle repeating pattern we mentioned earlier—the double helix of seeing with love and acting from the heart, which, when they occur at the right place and the right time, produce these miracles of greatness.

The moment of seeing with love, seeing with compassionate vision, has almost nothing to do with thinking. In fact, over time it became clear to us that thinking is actually an obstacle to this kind of seeing. The actor in the situation seems to see in an instant from the heart. In that instant of seeing, a sudden transformation happens.

CHAPTER SEVEN

SEEING AS A TRANSFORMATIVE ACT

There were many people on the subway platform on that January day in New York, but it was Wesley Autrey who saw the possibility for immediate and lifesaving action. There were other teachers and administrators in the college where Bart McGettrick was principal, but he was the one who envisioned the way forward for the girl and her unborn son that provided her with a sense of dignity. There were billions of witnesses to apartheid, but it was Nelson Mandela and Frederik W. de Klerk who saw the possibility for healing and forgiveness among the races. Humberto Maturana finds seeing and loving to be linked:

"If I look at the biology, when you [truly] see, you stop interposing prejudices, demands, and theories between you and what appears. Then you see what appears and you act according to what you see. When you act according to what you see, you are responsible. You cannot escape (responsibility) when you act according to what you see.

"Suppose I am driving my car in Santiago. I come to a red light and stop. As I stop, a child appears in the window asking for money. When faced with this, I can react in two or three different ways. I can say, 'Oh, there is so much misery nowadays in Santiago.' If I say, 'Misery has increased so much, and this government has caused these conditions,' I see not the child, but my theory about government as the source of the misery. However, it is not misery in front of me; it is a child. If I say, 'Oh my goodness, this could be my child,' in this case, I see the child. If I don't interpose the theory, I see the child. Then I will ask, 'What am I doing to bring forth a world in which this happens?' If you let the child appear, that is the act of love. Then you see and you cannot escape the emotion that the scene evokes in you, and you become aware of it."

Dadi Janki also speaks of the direct link between the attitude of love and a vision of the other that transforms: "Let me have an attitude and a vision of brotherhood. When I remain in the awareness of myself as a soul, I see each one as a soul, my brother. Whatever is in my attitude will be revealed through my eyes. This is why, when there is a soul-conscious stage, and I look at the other as a soul, I see them with love and compassion."

A clear case of seeing the other with elevated vision is the story of Father Ceyrac, who expressed the idea in terms of beauty:

> I think beauty is God's reflection of the world. The beauty of the children . . . you see God in them. If we want to love somebody, we must see the beauty of that person. We love beauty by nature. We are meant for beauty.
>
> Suppose a boy loves a girl. For him the girl is the most beautiful in the world, even if the nose is [*he makes a motion indicating a crooked nose*]. Love makes you see the beauty, and when you see the beauty, you love more.
>
> When I bless a marriage, I say that you must see the beauty of one another every day. The greatest problem is that we don't see the beauty of people. The beauty is extraordinary. When we see the beauty of people, there is no problem left. We love them.
>
> When a student group comes to India, I give an introduction. The first thing to see when you come to India—for God's sake, don't see the poverty, like an old colonizer. Don't see the poverty. Don't see that. See the beauty of the people. When you see the tremendous beauty of the people of India, then you see India. Poverty is a different thing.

Father Ceyrac's vision of India explains his extraordinary contribution there. For more than seventy years he has worked feverishly—intoxicated with his love for the beautiful children of India. He didn't labor from the burdened sense of duty that might have come from the vision of "an old colonizer." He worked in the lightness and joy of his love for the beautiful children in front of him.

But seeing with elevated vision is not always a natural experience. One of the most poignant moments of our interviews was when Hafsat Abiola talked about the man who betrayed her father in Nigeria:

> I get very angry. There are certain things that make me very angry. I think my husband sometimes is shocked. How I can be so loving in one moment, and then get very angry in the next? When I think of my father and how he was betrayed by some of his closest friends—especially the one who was the real Judas among all of them . . . You've never seen such a change in a person, as happened in this man. It disappoints me. And I get very disappointed in myself. I have thought before about the time when I could walk up to this man in a room and extend my hand to him in forgiveness and really mean it. But I cannot do that. I really feel concerned about the limitations that I possess, how swift I am to be like a lioness protecting a cub. I can be overwhelmed by the anger inside.

Maturana was especially thoughtful about this story from Hafsat Abiola:

"It may happen that if she did go to this man and tell him, 'I know that you betrayed my father, but I have no anger anymore. I have lived and see that the world is changing. Because this is the only thing that you could do in that moment, you did it. For the peace of my soul and for the harmony of my living, I wish you well.'

"What would this man think? He may think, 'Oh my goodness—she knows that I did this, and I believe in her sincerity. What is this? I don't think she is a hypocrite.' So this action would touch him. And what would be seen and remembered would be an act of greatness—an honest person attempting to go beyond a very painful situation.

"Because what you would see as greatness would be her action—not the result—regardless of what happens. An observer would likely notice that she was generous of spirit, of soul. In that act, she would free herself of her resentment.

"It is very possible that this would happen in a moment when she could be heard by him and, as a result, he would be changed—not because she wanted a certain outcome, but because her words came from respect.

"She would like to do this, but it cannot be done, because at this time she does not have the intrinsic inner harmony. If she said, 'Okay, I forgive you. I just wanted to liberate myself,' she is not freed from resentment. If you forgive with anger, you do not forgive. You have to forget. Forgiveness occurs when you forget. By forget, I mean forget even the emotion that holds you."

Dadi Janki sounded a similar note in her reflections on forgiveness: "The same ones who have brought us sorrow or anger will come in front of us one day to be forgiven. Holding on to the fact that someone has betrayed or deceived us makes us hostage to the anger inside. In fact, we should also help the ones who have deceived us to forget that they have done this to us. When we see the opportunity for forgiveness, we have to help them reduce their pain and suffering, which is the consequence of the earlier actions they took. This is why we need to have forgiveness, love, mercy, and compassion. To help someone forget their own misdeeds is the highest form of charity."

CHAPTER EIGHT

ACTING FROM THE HEART

W hile many who are visible on the world stage
make sweeping, deliberate actions filled with
an awareness of themselves as the leader or
even the hero in the situation, in the cases of what we are
calling greatness, the exact opposite seems to occur. All sense
of identity of "I" as the one who is doing this action virtually
evaporates as the person moves into action. His or her focus
remains fixed on the person at the center of the situation and
the needs of the moment. When the situation calls for it, he
or she moves quickly with no wasted effort, doing exactly
what the moment requires without thinking of resources,
obstacles, or repercussions.

The stories have a remarkable similarity. It is as if the path forward, which is invisible to anyone else on the scene, is absolutely clear to the person who acts. They move with a sureness and an accuracy that cannot be explained by any subsequent logic. They seem to know exactly what they must do in that moment. If Bart McGettrick had begun to weigh the repercussions of going against college policy . . . if Wesley Autrey had begun to think about the very small clearance under the New York subway tracks and his daughters on the platform . . . if Father Ceyrac had stopped to calculate the cost of caring for the orphans in India and the improbability of their ever really getting out of poverty, the opportunity for greatness would have been lost.

It is as if their loving vision opens an otherwise invisible door to a path of opportunity, and on the other side of that door is a subtle corridor leading in a direction that no one else can see. When that door opens, they surrender their ego and sense of "I," putting themselves in service to something higher. They do not think in our traditional notion of that word; rather, they move along hyperalert, calm, and very efficient, guided from one moment to the next through the experience. They are moving in the state of "instrument consciousness," described earlier by Dadi Janki. This state is captured in *Star Wars* when young Luke Skywalker is steering his spaceship in perilous circumstances, trying to read the instruments to guide his way. He hears the voice of Obi-Wan

Kenobi saying, "The force, Luke. Use the force," at which point he stops thinking and surrenders to some subtle guidance that takes over and steers the spacecraft to a successful mission.

Maturana described one such moment in his own life, with his wife, Beatriz:

"I was once Superman. The story of my being Superman was as follows: We were going up a hill holding hands in a line, I first, Beatriz next, and then her mother, Yolanda. Her mother released Beatriz's hand to hold on to a branch in a nearby tree, but she failed to grasp the branch and began falling down the hill. Beatriz quickly released my hand, fell to her knees, and began to pray. As I looked at what was happening, I turned and did three consecutive jumps down the hill, placing myself below Yolanda, and received her in my arms. She was a slim lady, some eighty-two years old, and was not very heavy. When I did this, I did not stop to think what to do or how to do what I had to do. In a look, I was fully aware of the whole situation. To put it another way, in that look I took in the whole system of what was unfolding and instantly knew what I should do and how I should do it. I knew that I had to go beyond her and catch her before her second turn downhill, conscious that if I did not do that, she would roll down to certain death. I jumped with total precision on a slippery surface downhill and caught her in my arms. When I placed Yolanda safely on the ground, I apologized to her, because my right hand had rested on her breast without her permission. She smiled and gave me a kiss. Afterward I marveled at what I had done, realizing that if I had stopped to think about what I should do, I would not have caught her.

"Instantly seeing the whole system of which you are a part is what is special in a situation like this. Systemic seeing occurs only when you are seeing with love. The systemic seeing of love occurs only when there are no interfering emotions that make your purposes or desires guide what you do. As love becomes the unconscious guide of your doings, you see the systemic relational-operational matrix of which you are a part and in which you are immersed. You immediately know how to move in it. Seeing with love is not seeing with goodness, or kindness, or goodwill, or generosity—it is just systemic seeing. When we act in a moment of systemic seeing, we act with care for the circumstances we are in at the moment, and according to what we see that is adequate to do there and then."

Or consider this story about Brooke Rodgers, a sixteen-year-old girl in Chicago. She hoped to have a summer job as a lifeguard, and so in preparation for that, she had taken a course in first aid from the American Red Cross. A few months after she finished her course, she had the opportunity to use what she had learned.

I was on the second floor of school and looked out the window on the intersection below. There was a woman in the crosswalk, and as I was watching, a car hit her. I saw her fly up in the air, and then I saw her hit the ground. I dropped my bag and ran down the stairs. When I got to the crosswalk, someone was standing near the woman to make sure no car hit her, but no one was talking to her. Two waitresses from the restaurant on the corner were outside on the sidewalk looking. I asked them to call 911. Then I walked up to her and knelt beside her. I remembered the part of my training that said you should introduce yourself and ask if you can help them. So I told her my name was Brooke, and I asked her if I could help her. She nodded yes. She was looking right at me. I knew that she had hit her head by the way she fell. I started to do the primary and secondary steps of the first aid training, in which you ask the person how they are and check to see if they have hurt themselves. I knew she [had] hit her head, but I also knew she might not be aware of any other part of her that was hurt. So I patted her down and realized that she had also hurt her leg. About that time the waitresses came out with two blankets and said that emergency medical service [EMS] was on the way. I told the woman EMS was on the way and that someone was directing traffic around her. EMS was very fast. When they showed up, I told them that she had hit her head and that her leg was probably broken too. They put her in the ambulance. She looked directly at me and said, "Thank you, Brooke." Then they drove away.

I guess what I remember the most, the thing that was remarkable to me, was that once you have the training, you just do what you know you should do. I didn't become aware of what I should do until after it was over.

Maturana, in leaping to his mother-in-law's aid, and Rodgers, in rushing to help the woman in the crosswalk, report the same phenomenon as the other actors we have interviewed and read about. By the time they moved to action, some inner transformation seems to have already happened. Rodgers described the experience as "sort of a moment of internal silence." Lenny Skutnik, the federal employee who leaped into the icy Potomac after the Air Florida flight, used almost the same words: "It was very quiet—that eerie quiet when it snows . . . and out of the quiet, this woman was yelling for help: 'Will somebody please help?'"

It is as if in those moments, consciousness of the world falls away and the actor and those they are helping are in a suspended moment together, a moment beyond logic and thinking, an unscheduled moment that plays out perfectly in ways they cannot explain later. In fact, the actions are such that later the hero actors claim no responsibility for what happened and often express sheer gratitude and happiness at having been the one who was there to help.

Rodgers, in reflecting on her experience, said:

> I was really surprised that she remembered my name. My thought was that if you were caught up in an experience like that, you would be thinking about what had happened to you. I know even when nothing has happened to me, I don't necessarily remember a person's name when they introduce themselves. So I took it as another sign that the training was really good—that they created the training in response to what they know about how a person feels when they are in a situation like that.
>
> . . . It was a moment that was uplifting, because I could quit fretting over the tedious mundane stuff and just do what I knew I needed to do.

The day after his heroic save in the subway, a *New York Times* reporter asked Wesley Autrey to reflect on what had happened. At the end of the interview, after recounting the whole sequence of what had happened, he simply said, "Maybe I was in the right place at the right time, and good things happen for good people."

CHAPTER NINE

THE RIPPLE EFFECT
OF GREATNESS

Psychology academics have extensively documented the negative effects on those witnessing violence and calamity. Volumes have been written on post-traumatic stress syndrome and other biological effects on those who witness acts of terror. Less studied, but equally important, is the subject of what happens to those who witness acts of greatness. One pioneer in this research is Jonathan Haidt, professor of psychology at the University of Virginia. He says, "In my work on the moral emotions, I have stumbled upon a class of emotions that is almost completely unstudied: the emotions we feel when other people

69

do good, skillful, or admirable things. These emotions are unusual in that they are not primarily about ourselves, our goals, and our normal petty concerns. These emotions give people a sense of uplift and inspiration; they make us feel like better people; they are self-transcendent."

One of the first such emotions that Haidt studied in this class of "other praising emotions" was an emotion called elevation: "Elevation is a warm, uplifting feeling that people experience when they see unexpected acts of human goodness, kindness, and compassion. It makes a person want to help others and to become a better person himself or herself."

In Haidt's research the circumstances that most often caused people to experience elevation involved seeing someone else give help to another in need. Here is one of the stories Haidt and his team came across in their research:

"Myself and three guys from my church were going home from volunteering our services at the Salvation Army that morning. It had been snowing since the night before and the snow was a thick blanket on the ground. As we were driving through a neighborhood near where I lived, I saw an elderly woman with a shovel in her driveway. I did not think much of it, when one of the guys in the back asked the driver to let him off here. The driver had not been paying much attention so he ended up circling back around towards the lady's home. I assumed that this guy just wanted to save the driver some effort and walk the short distance to his home (although I was clueless as to where he lived). But when I saw him jump out of the back seat and approach the lady, my mouth dropped in shock as I realized that he was offering to shovel her walk for her.

"My spirit was lifted even higher than it already was. I was joyous, happy, smiling, energized. I went home and gushed about it to my suite-mates, who clutched at their hearts. And, although I have never seen this guy as more than just a friend, I felt a hint of romantic feeling for him at this moment."

Haidt did many studies on elevation, asking subjects to think of a specific time when they saw a manifestation of humanity's "higher" or "better" nature. One such study involved showing subjects video clips of Mother Teresa working with the poor in Calcutta. These studies were not confined to the United States. In Orissa, India, he conducted eight interviews in a small village, asking informants to discuss potentially emotional situations they had experienced, one of which was a "time when you saw someone do something wonderful, a very good deed, to someone else, but not to you." Six of the informants described clear cases of witnessing a good deed, and in all six cases the hallmarks of elevation were present (i.e., warm, tingly feelings, positive affect, and a motivation to help others).

A Japanese American student of Haidt's conducted similar interviews with fifteen people from varied backgrounds in

Japan. She found that informants were emotionally respon-
sive to the good deeds of others in ways that resembled the
responses of Americans and Indians. Informants described a
variety of situations that moved their hearts, such as seeing
a gang member giving up his seat on the train to an elderly
person, seeing news about Mother Teresa, and watching the
band in the movie Titanic playing on courageously as the
ship sank. For example, when interviewing a forty-six-year-
old housewife, the following exchange took place.

Q: Have you ever had positive feelings due to something
   others did?
A: Yes I have. For example, when there is a natural disaster in another country, those who actually go there and
   help people as volunteers. Also those who do things
   within [their limits], such as collecting money and food
   and clothes for those who are suffering from disaster.
Q: You feel positive feelings when you hear stories about
   those people?
A: Yes.
Q: Can you explain in detail?
A: I wonder if there is anything that I can do with my own
   strength. For example, donating money, giving clothes,
   and I have done that before myself . . . I think how I
   could join those people even though what I have done
   is not much compared to what they do.

Q: When you have these feelings, do you have any physical feeling?

A: When I see news of a disaster, I feel pain in my chest, and tears actually come out when I read the newspaper. Then after that, seeing volunteers and finding out that they are helping people out there, the pain goes away, the heart brightens up [akarui] and I feel glad [sonkei], relieved [anshin], admiration [sugoi], and respect [sonkei]. When I see volunteers, the heart heavy from sad news becomes lighter.

In these Japanese interviews, as in the Indian interviews, the same elements are conjoined: The perception of compassionate or courageous behavior by others causes a pleasurable physical feeling in the chest of movement, warmth, or opening, coupled with a desire to engage in virtuous action oneself. (Haidt, *Flourishing*, 282–83)

We found evidence to support Haidt's claim in our own research when we came across Zilda Arns Neumann, a Brazilian pediatrician who founded and leads Pastoral da Criança (the Pastoral of the Child), an innovative public health program that works with more than 265,000 volunteers in 42,000 pastoral communities in Brazil to combat poverty, disease, hunger, illiteracy, and injustice. Neumann has won countless awards for her work and was nominated for a Nobel Peace Prize in 2005. Her account of what inspired her to become a physician and educator in service to the poor is a demonstration of the findings of Haidt and his colleagues concerning the effects of witnessing humanity's higher nature:

> I was born in Forquilhinha, a southern village in the Brazilian state of Santa Catarina. I am the twelfth child among 13 sisters and brothers. We were part of a rural community, provided with an excellent primary school, and excellent parish of Franciscan friars, and an excellent library for local families. My parents, who had seven daughters, wanted all their girls to be dedicated to studies. So, they built a house in Curitiba, which was already renowned as a university city. In Curitiba, we used to go to the Congregation of Franciscan Friars, where we could find excellent books and movies. I was impressed in a singular way by two movies on missionaries who went to Amazonia. Those pictures of missionary doctors working with destitute people with malaria, who were lying in beds trembling with fever, touched me deeply. Then, we watched another movie showing missionary doctors working in the slums with children who spent their days playing in sewers. I decided: I'm going to be a doctor and I will become a missionary.

Had she not been inspired by the movies of the missionaries working in the Amazon, Neumann may have simply gone on to become a successful pediatrician in Brazil. However, touched and inspired by what she saw, she chose a very different life as a pediatrician, educator, and philanthropist. We asked her to reflect on her choice. She said:

> It is an intimate pleasure one feels when called on to help others. It's a vocation: one feels attracted when one hears a call. It's a feeling of being an instrument—to use that which we have—personal education, professional expertise, talents, faith, abundance of the heart. I felt that all of these are divine gifts, given to us so that we can share them with others. One feels all of this can be shared in a way that will bring happiness to others.

Haidt concluded that "Love and affiliation appear to be a common human response to witnessing saints and saintly deeds, or even to hearing about them second hand." Neumann's choice to become a missionary doctor, like those in the Amazon that she had seen on the movies in the library of the Franciscan friars, is an example of this desire for love and affiliation with those who do saintly deeds.

Another psychology researcher has drawn the world's attention to the way that experiencing positive emotions actually builds our reserves and broadens our capacities. Barbara Fredrickson, a psychology professor at the University of North Carolina, reframed the way the world thought about positive emotions with her important 1998 article, "What Good are Positive Emotions?" In this article she laid out a theory of positive emotion that she called "the broaden-and-build theory": "This theory states that certain discrete positive emotions . . . share the ability to broaden people's momentary thought-action repertoires and build their enduring personal resources, ranging from physical and intellectual resources to social and psychological resources. The broadened thought-action repertoires triggered by positive emotions carry indirect and long-term adaptive benefits. They broaden the scopes of attention, cognition, and action and build physical, intellectual, and social resources—enduring personal resources, which function as reserves to be drawn on later to manage future threats" (Fredrickson, *American Psychologist* [March 2001]: 219–20). Haidt observed, "Elevation seemed to open people up and turn their attention outward, toward other people. Elevation therefore fits well with Fredrickson's (1998) 'broaden-and-build' model of the positive emotions, in which positive emotions are said to motivate people to cultivate skills and relationships that will help them in the long run" (Haidt, *Flourishing*, 282).

If Haidt, Fredrickson, and others who are studying the effect of witnessing—or even hearing about—acts of kindness and generosity are right, their findings have huge implications for ways to transform societies from patterns of apathy, anger, and fear to patterns of generosity, courage, and affiliation with others. Of course, the groundswells of support for leaders like Gandhi and Martin Luther King Jr. are well documented, but there is evidence of the ways that people are moved and uplifted by the more isolated acts of greatness as well.

The *New York Times* article on the subway hero reported what happened to Wesley Autrey after his heroic save:

Mr. Autrey, a 50-year-old construction worker, said he knew something was different when he showed up for work later on Tuesday. His boss, he said, bought him lunch—a ham-and-cheese hero—and later told him to take the day off.

Then yesterday morning, as he walked to his mother's apartment in Harlem, "a stranger came up and put $10 in my hand," he said. "People in my neighborhood were like, 'Yo, I know this guy.'"

Once at his mother's apartment, he held interviews in the living room with some of the national morning news programs.

After that, it was back to the scene, where he recounted Mr. Hollopeter's backward tumble off the platform and into the path of the oncoming train.

Throughout the day, Mr. Autrey's sister, Linda, 48, played the role of administrative assistant, logging invitations for the talk-show circuit, including requests from the David Letterman, Charlie Rose and Ellen DeGeneres shows. Phone calls from well-wishers came pouring in, including one from the mayor's office. Mr. Autrey said he had been offered cash, trips and scholarships for his two daughters, Syshe, 4, and Shuqui, 6, who watched as he dived to the trackbed.

"Donald Trump's got a check waiting on me," he said. "They offered to mail it; I said, 'No, I'd like to meet the Donald, so I can say, Yo, you're fired.'"

By the end of the day, the president of the New York Film Academy, Jerry Sherlock, had personally handed him a $5,000 check.

We asked Maturana to reflect on the outpouring of generosity that happens spontaneously when people witness acts of kindness, courage, and love: "Loving acts inspire loving acts. Trust inspires trust. Anger inspires anger. So if one person is honest, other people will see his or her honesty and will be touched by it and inspired to act on that.

Witnessing these kinds of acts inspires great debates: 'How can this be?' It concerns others, because it has to do with them too. Each one asks, 'Could I have done this?' In the case when someone is able to forgive a horrible act, others ask themselves, 'Could I have forgiven such a horrible thing? Now that I think about it, how could I sustain my anger, now that I have seen this kind of forgiveness?' This is an interesting thing—that those who witness acts of courage, generosity, or exceptional forgiveness are deeply affected by what they have seen."

We asked Dadi Janki about the ripple effect of greatness. She said:

"When your intent is pure, it has a vibrant impact on others. When you are touched by a good quality—inspired by a virtue or a value—and act in an elevated way, your action has the potential to inspire others. It is a natural law that souls respond to the quality of intention they experience in others. When we speak about inspiration, this is what we are speaking about. Many things cannot be done without inspiration. If you have inspiration, you find the courage and strength you need, and nothing can stop you.

"So, when someone witnesses an act of goodness, an act done entirely without self-interest, they are transformed by the purity of intention in that act. They may feel admiration, or they may feel gratitude. These feelings of admiration and gratitude are really blessings. These blessings flow out from the person who is seeing the good action as pure wishes for the one who is performing the elevated action. There is double reward in this—blessings for the one doing the action and inspiration and courage arising in the one who is witnessing the action."

We are reminded of the observation Tex Gunning made on greatness early in our research: that we are moved by contact with greatness, because it is innate in us.

CHAPTER TEN

CULTIVATING GREATNESS

G reatness is not something we can prepare for in the way we study for an exam. In virtually all domains of life—from baseball to warfare and from investment banking to television production—we are encouraged to think, to analyze, and to plan. Successful action, we are told, will result from this. Promotions and power come to those who think the most, analyze accurately, and plan well. But in the realm we are referring to as "something beyond greatness," the premium is not on thinking, analyzing, and planning.

Those who are blessed with the fortune of serving others—whether in a moment or over a lifetime—appear to be lifted beyond the gravitational pull of thinking and taking planned steps. The instant they see the other with an elevated vision of love, the bonds that tied them to cautious thinking and planning fall away, and they move to a state of knowing in the heart what they must do. They act with sureness and ease and then afterward savor the state of grace in which they find themselves.

In scrutinizing the stories we found in our search and seeking to make meaning out of them, we concluded that this phenomenon of greatness is beyond analysis. In the same way that you can't teach someone how to fall in love, you can't teach someone how to have a life that is filled with greatness. It is not teachable, but it may be learnable.

Maturana contends that it is our nature to be loving beings. He believes we lose touch with our natural, loving nature when we try to assert our will on things, when we try to get others to meet our expectations—to do what we want them to do. He says, "We human beings are fundamentally loving beings. Something happens when you see the legitimacy of the other. Love just sees, and then you act according to what you see. If you let the other be, the other will appear in their legitimacy and you will act accordingly." He suggests we simply watch others in the "doings of their lives," and as we watch them with this appreciation, we will natu-

READER/CUSTOMER CARE SURVEY

We care about your opinions! Please take a moment to fill out our online Reader Survey at **http://survey.hcibooks.com**.

As a **"THANK YOU"** you will receive a **VALUABLE INSTANT COUPON** towards future book purchases as well as a **SPECIAL GIFT** available only online! Or, you may mail this card back to us.

(PLEASE PRINT IN ALL CAPS)

First Name		MI.	Last Name	

Address				

State	Zip		Email	City

1. Gender
- ❑ Female
- ❑ Male

2. Age
- ❑ 8 or younger
- ❑ 9-12
- ❑ 13-16
- ❑ 17-20
- ❑ 21-30
- ❑ 31+

3. Did you receive this book as a gift?
- ❑ Yes
- ❑ No

4. Annual Household Income
- ❑ under $25,000
- ❑ $25,000 - $34,999
- ❑ $35,000 - $49,999
- ❑ $50,000 - $74,999
- ❑ over $75,000

5. What are the ages of the children living in your house?
- ❑ 0 - 14
- ❑ 15+

6. Marital Status
- ❑ Single
- ❑ Married
- ❑ Divorced
- ❑ Widowed

7. How did you find out about the book?
(please choose one)
- ❑ Recommendation
- ❑ Store Display
- ❑ Online
- ❑ Catalog/Mailing
- ❑ Interview/Review

8. Where do you usually buy books?
(please choose one)
- ❑ Bookstore
- ❑ Online
- ❑ Book Club/Mail Order
- ❑ Price Club (Sam's Club, Costco's, etc.)
- ❑ Retail Store (Target, Wal-Mart, etc.)

9. What subject do you enjoy reading about the most?
(please choose one)
- ❑ Parenting/Family
- ❑ Relationships
- ❑ Recovery/Addictions
- ❑ Health/Nutrition
- ❑ Christianity
- ❑ Spirituality/Inspiration
- ❑ Business Self-help
- ❑ Women's Issues
- ❑ Sports

10. What attracts you most to a book?
(please choose one)
- ❑ Title
- ❑ Cover Design
- ❑ Author
- ❑ Content

TAPE IN MIDDLE; DO NOT STAPLE

FOLD HERE

Comments

rally be moved to act in a loving way. To make his point about the natural emergence of our loving nature, he recounted the classic story of Faust:

Have you read Goethe's *Faust*? Faust is an interesting middle-aged, mythic personage who sells his soul to the devil. When this happens in stories, the devil provides you with something of worldly value, such as fame or riches, in exchange for your soul. There are different stories about this. In some of these stories the devil takes the soul; in others, the human being manages to cheat the devil; sometimes they are helped by a woman, by love. The devil never cheats. He always fulfills his part of the bargain, but the human beings are always trying to cheat. In the story by Goethe, this Faust is an alchemist, a magician, an old professor at a university, but he is bored to death. Nothing touches him. Life has no meaning. Suddenly the devil appears and offers to show Faust the secrets of the world and let him experience the profoundest pleasures. In return, when Faust dies, he must surrender his immortal soul to the devil. Faust agrees on one condition: the adventure must culminate in a moment when he experiences the highest, most exquisite pleasure attainable by man. The devil agrees to this offer and makes Faust young again. He goes on adventures with bandits, seduces a young woman named Margarita, who falls in love with him, and becomes a leader in war. Toward the end of Faust's life, the devil importunes him to embark on another adventure, one filled with earthly pleasure. But Faust seeks a higher challenge, and he can think of none better than to reclaim land from the sea and put it to productive use. So, he begins to develop an enterprise of taking land from the sea and building houses for people. There is a moment when he becomes so exalted by what he's doing to benefit humankind that he says, "Oh moment, stop!" In this instant the devil shows up to collect.

Maturana's point in recalling the story of Faust is that the highest, most exquisite pleasure attainable by man turns out not to be the earthly pleasures of adventure and seduction. The most exquisite pleasure comes to Faust only when he becomes consumed in the natural act of loving and giving to others. It is through loving that he is redeemed. It is this exalted state that defines the kind of greatness we are talking about—the natural state of being in harmony with the most elevated qualities in ourselves and of giving naturally and spontaneously to those around us.

Some have the good fortune of having easy access to their natural, loving nature, while others of us have lost touch with this part of ourselves. Earlier we shared Maturana's story about driving in Santiago and having a poor child come up to the car-begging. He suggested that there are two possible responses to the child: (1) see the theory of government's failure to care for the poor or (2) see the child. Those of us who have lost touch with the wellspring of love within us will not see the child and will lose the opportunity to serve with a vision of love.

How do we return to our original loving nature to reclaim greatness in ourselves? How would those who aspire to greatness find the door that opens into the corridor that leads to greatness? Dadi Janki suggests that it is about remembering: "Each one has original and eternal qualities that are like God's. God is our Mother, our Father, and we have those same eternal qualities of love, peace, happiness, and power within us. But we have forgotten who we are. Over time we have come under the influence of the world. We have become distracted by desires for material things and attached to the people and things of the world. We have had experiences that caused us to feel sorrow, anger, and fear. As this has happened to us, we have gradually forgotten our original, loving nature. The door to our eternal self has quietly closed, and we have found ourselves alone. We do not need to feel alone. We do not need to remain in the dark."

If we have never known something, we must learn it from someone who knows, but if something was ours to begin with, then we can claim it again by remembering. So it is with Raja Yoga, the spiritual practice that Dadi Janki follows. "Raja" is the Hindi word for sovereign or king, and "Yoga" is the Hindi word for yoke or link. Raja Yoga is a spiritual practice through which one reclaims the natural sovereignty of the self through remembrance. So we asked Dadi Janki, in Raja Yoga, what do we remember? She responded:

"First, we remember who we are and then who we belong to. I am a soul, an eternal being of light, and I am a child of the Supreme Soul; I am a child of God. To remember my Supreme Parent, I need to go beyond sound into silence. The practice of staying beyond sound is absolutely essential. Silence is the language of the soul. In deep silence I turn my attention from me, the soul, to God, the being of light who is my eternal parent, and I become lost in remembrance. In this space of deep, silent remembrance, I forge a relationship, and I experience God's love. This love from God evokes my own natural, loving nature. When this love fills my awareness, my attitude becomes benevolent, and when my attitude is benevolent, I naturally see with loving eyes. I see those around me not as 'the other,' but as a brother or sister, as one who belongs to me."

This is Wesley Autrey in the New York subway. It is Bart McGettrick in the school in Scotland. It is Father Ceyrac with his children in India. And it is countless parents and neighbors and citizens around the world who engage in quiet acts of love and generosity that we never hear about.

CHAPTER ELEVEN

SOMETHING BEYOND
GREATNESS

A s we observed earlier, emotional and psychological states are contagious. They spread through
societies like a fire through a parched forest. This
is true whether the state is anger or love. Wesley Autrey
didn't just save Cameron Hollopeter that day on the subway
platform in New York; he kindled a light of possibility for
the thousands of people who heard his story. This is true of
all of the men and women who we talked about here—of
Father Ceyrac in India, of Bart McGettrick in Scotland, and
of Hafsat Abiola in Nigeria. What the world needs now is
not only individual moments of greatness or even individual

lives of greatness, but whole communities of greatness. We need to move beyond admiring greatness in the other to becoming like that ourselves. Each of us has everything we need inside—the love, the peace, and the generosity of spirit we see in these great ones.

In the course of working on this book, we sat with Dadi Janki in India and asked her about those who everyone considers to be great, such as Mahatma Gandhi. She responded thoughtfully:

"Yes, Gandhi was able to liberate India using nonviolent means. But remember this was not his highest aim. His goal was to create 'Ramraj,' to create heaven on earth. This he was not able to do. He made so much effort to get independence for the people of India. But since then, corruption, competition, and divisiveness have actually increased. The people of India honored his life principles, but only in theory. They turned him into an icon, but in their day-to-day lives, they turned their backs on what he was saying. They forgot the disciplines he upheld to attain his elevated level of consciousness. He had led a life that he described as 'experiments with truth,' in which he was intentionally seeking the highest truths. He became very simple, and for a while he was able to inspire others to be like him, but he was not able to create a sustained community of great ones. This is what we need at this time—not for one person to be great, but to create communities of greatness."

Maturana reflected on the mythic history of King Arthur, the figure at the center of the Arthurian legends and the designer of an order of the best knights of the world in Camelot: "It did not work because of ambition, betrayal, and competition. It worked for a while, but then came the love affair between Lancelot and Guinevere and the treachery of Arthur's son, Mordred. Those are the ambitions and weaknesses that destroyed it. Then living together in mutual respect became difficult. What one would like to happen is that there could be a community in which people live together in a collaboration through which they conserve honesty and self-respect. All of these things have been understood by humanity. It is understood that the experiment in Camelot failed, but the attempt will be remembered."

We asked Maturana whether there is something special about our times, something that would allow us not to repeat these mistakes again. He said:

"We know practically everything we need to know. Our problem is to be willing to act in accordance with that, for the benefit of the human being. We have the means, but we need the will. For example, there is a theme, which is population growth. If the population goes on growing and growing, there is no possibility. There is a long history in biology of what happens when a population grows unchecked; there is disaster. It grows faster than the environment can accommodate.

We know this. Are we willing to take the whole complex network of actions so the population growth diminishes and the population becomes stable? There are theories and doctrines against this. Those espousing these theories and doctrines say they are protecting life. Are they protecting life? Or are they protecting procreation? If we do not act in accordance with the understanding that this is something we must do, there is not a chance for humanity. In this moment we know what we need to do. We have the means, but we need the will."

We asked Maturana to say more about the will. "The will is the passion that we put into doing what we want to do," he explained. "As we act in life, we reveal that we do not have the will to do what we claim we want to do. Our actions show that we do not [really] want to do that thing: that we want something else more. Reason does not guide human behavior, emotions guide human behavior." In other words, while we human beings may say that we want something to change—say, global warming—when it comes to actually acting in such a way as to make a change, we do not really have the determination, the will, to act in that way. We continue to act in a way to get what we want more—comfort, for example—even if logic and reasoning tell us there may be disastrous consequences for continuing our old way of acting.

Maturana explained further, "We human beings claim to be rational beings, but it is not so. We are emotional beings who use reason to justify our emotional responses. Our desires give us energy for acting. We apply our energy in the domains in which we have desires."

This is what distinguishes greatness. The great ones we studied consistently acted beyond self-interest and comfort to benefit a larger whole. They gave up their lives—some literally—and put themselves in service to the other. These acts of love set them apart from all of the rest of humanity. But at this time, the world needs collective greatness, not just individual greatness. It is not necessary for everyone to act in this transcendent way, but it does seem necessary for a critical mass to have this kind of will, this kind of dedication to something higher than their own desires, if we are to harness our collective greatness.

We asked Dadi Janki the same question we asked Maturana: "Is there something special about this time, something that will allow us not to make the mistakes of the past again?"

She replied, "Yes, *kaliyug* [the age of darkness] is coming to an end, and *satyug* [the age of truth] is coming. This is the time in between. This is the time when it is possible for us to know our true selves, to know God, and to have a relationship with God. We human beings cannot create a community of greatness. Even individual great ones like Gandhi and Mandela could not do this. But God can do this, and that is the task of this time. He accomplishes this task by awakening us, by showing us who we really are. At the same time that much of the world is in darkness, the first light of the new world is breaking."

Dadi Janki returned to the subject of love: "The secret to this awakening is breaking our bondage to our limited physical bodies and experiencing ourselves to be the unlimited being inside, the soul. In this soul-consciousness we remember God and feel the closeness of belonging to Him. This flow of love between me, the soul, and God gives me attainments I never thought possible—for example, courage and the will or determination that Humberto [Maturana] spoke about."

What Dadi Janki explained was the holy grail of the search for something beyond greatness. The reason that our longing for greatness in the world generally exceeds our grasp is that we are trapped in limited understandings of who we are. Though King Arthur's knights may have been the best knights in the world, their efforts were made from the limited awareness of being physical human beings. They became entangled in their own selfish desires and couldn't summon the will or the inner strength to act for the benefit of all of Camelot.

Dadi Janki's confidence about the future comes from her personal relationship with God and the strength and clarity she takes from that. She believes that at this time, if we are to move beyond isolated moments of greatness and individual lives of greatness to create a community of greatness in the world, we have to draw on our unlimited identity of ourselves and on the endless well of God's power. Dadi Janki reminded us of something we had considered earlier—the ripple effect of greatness. She said, "We talk about how science, technology, and media have made this world a global village. There is a kind of sharing that causes the world to be global. One bird from Asia can bring a flu to the rest of the world. The same thing can happen with the spreading of a change of awareness. When enough people begin to experience themselves and humanity in a way that is not limited by the physical world, in the unlimited way that God sees us, the world will reach a tipping point and will tip into an age of truth."

CHAPTER TWELVE

REFLECTIONS ON THE SEARCH FOR GREATNESS

At the end of our search, we concluded that what an observer sees when he or she witnesses greatness is love. Love appears as the foundation of greatness in human behavior. We listened to sociologists, biologists, mystics, educators, and politicians, and regardless of whether they referred to the inspiration of the Divine or to our biology as human beings to explain such behaviors, love always appeared as the foundation.

Love! What do we mean when we speak of love? Dadi Janki says that love is innate in the human soul and is awakened by God's grace, God's inspiration. When we act from a place of love, we accept the other as he or she is, seeing what is good in that one. Brazilian pediatrician, educator, and philanthropist Zilda Arns Neumann instinctively understood that her work was, at its root, about love. "I have satiated my need to love and be loved," she said. "A reporter in Germany once told me, 'You are the most important woman in Brazil.' And I replied to him, 'I am not the most important one, I am rather the most loved.'"

We asked Neumann what advice she would give to someone who came to her saying they wanted to dedicate their life to serving humanity. She replied, "Such a person has already gone halfway by even asking such a question. Now is the time to ponder how precious his/her life is. Life is a thing not to be wasted. Such a person must ponder over violence and inequality, over how much God means Love. Then they will experience the feeling that God has given them the capabilities to become an instrument of peace, justice, and solidarity. Love fulfills life."

Maturana says that we know we are observing love when we see someone behave in such a way that some other being arises as a "legitimate other" in coexistence with them. Both views, the scientific and the spiritual, agree that loving behavior arises through a fundamental inspiration ignited by the presence of love. In other words, we know a loving vision is present because we see the loving behavior that can only come from that loving vision.

Standing in stark contrast to this natural attitude of love and the systemic thinking it engenders is the kind of thinking, analyzing, and planning we spoke about earlier, which is the hallmark of ambition in all fields. Those who want success for themselves in any field—business, politics, sports, or academia—are generally told they must set goals and plan for that success. This counsel urges a narrowing of focus and what Maturana calls linear thinking:

"We live in a time and culture in which we cultivate, more than ever before, linear thinking and linear acting. We want success; we want efficiency; we want perfection; we want greatness; we want to win the war against poverty, hunger, or disease. But when we configure our thinking in such a linear way, we fail. Linear thinking, pursued to its extreme, unavoidably leads to the destruction of humanness, because it leads to the blind destruction of the systemic conditions of life—the biosphere and the anthroposphere that make human existence possible.

"Living beings are systemic entities. The cosmos, and the human beings that arise in it and generate it, as they explain their existence in it, are systemic entities. Linear processes unavoidably destroy all systemic processes when they take possession of them. Thus, the paths of linear thinking and linear actions in human life lead unavoidably to the dark Kali Yuga era of the Indian Vedic tradition."

Maturana is not making a religious, philosophical, or political statement. He is making a statement that arises from his understanding of the systemic nature of our biological existence, because systemic vision is the vision of love. Love is what makes systemic vision possible. He says that persistent linear thinking through any conviction, whether it is religious, philosophical, political, or scientific, whether it comes from a desire to advance high ideals or private gain, negates love. And when our thinking negates love, it negates systemic vision.

It is only a vision of love, a systemic vision, that allows one to take in the whole in a glance and to act spontaneously—sometimes in ways that we later can only explain as miracles. Linear thinking narrows the vision. When our vision narrows, the actions we take wreak havoc on the coherent interlacing of the systemic existence of human beings and the biosphere that supports life. We may not have intended to destroy these delicate, interlaced systems of life; it is just that in our narrowed focus on our goal, we never saw them.

Greatness is not an achievement. It is not something one obtains through dedicated effort. Greatness appears as an observer speaks of it, when he or she sees some human being acting spontaneously with systemic vision and is surprised or moved by the dramatic circumstances in which the action occurs. What the observer has, in fact, seen is not more and not less than the presence of love as the foundational emotion that moves, realizes, and conserves humanness.

We speak of greatness in human behavior when we see systemic vision in the form of a loving action. Loving vision and actions, systemic vision and systemic actions, are naturally there when we are not under the spell of some linear theory or linear argument that leads us into a path of linear thinking and acting. Linear thinking takes us away from the innocence and candor of our natural harmony with the loving connection, what Maturana would call the "systemic coherences" of the present moment in which we live. What an observer sees as greatness is simply acting in candor and innocence, doing what the present moment calls for. It is the candor and innocence of "letting be," the candor and innocence of forgetting greatness.

So if a loving vision is so natural, if candor and innocence are innate to the human being, why are they so rare? Why aren't actions like those of Wesley Autrey, Zilda Arns Neumann, and Bart McGettrick the norm? Why are they so unusual and moving that they merit our retelling and discussion? We asked Dadi Janki about this. She did what she often did when we asked her a question—she requested that we all take a few moments of silence together. When she emerged from silence, she carefully explained why special effort is required at this time:

"We are in a dark time, a time when the atmosphere and pressures of the world can create a feeling of heaviness in us and fill our minds with waste thoughts and negativity. What was once the natural nature of human beings—to be happy and at peace—is now unusual. In our lives, peace and happiness occur in fleeting moments that give us a glimpse of a dim light still flickering within us. It is remarkable that in the atmosphere of these times, a single loving moment can cause one to take a heroic action and to care for another in such a deep way. At this time, we need to fan the flame of this flickering inner light in the soul, so the darkness in the soul gives way to the light. Because the world has become filled with sadness, fear, and anger, the souls have absorbed these things, thus overshadowing the soul's natural, loving nature. We must learn to concentrate in a certain way to transform our inner world and reclaim our natural nature."

We asked her to say more about this. How is this kind of concentration different from the linear thinking that Maturana describes? She explained:

"Silence is the language of the soul, and in silence we awaken our divine insight. The power of silence comes from pure thoughts, good wishes, and soul-conscious vision for the other. The linear thinking that my brother Humberto talks about is based on the ego, on self-interest. The concentration I am speaking about within the power of silence comes when we are stable in our awareness of ourselves as the inner being, the immortal being of light. In this awareness, I naturally look at the other with a vision of love, and I become aware of what

I must do in any moment. The accurate thought about what I must do in the present arises as a touching or signal within. Great humility is required for this. I must maintain respect for the self, respect for the other, respect for the unfolding drama of life, and respect for God. We know we are acting in alignment with our natural nature because of the joy and happiness, the intoxication, we feel at that time."

On rereading what we have written, we must finally conclude that greatness is not so rare after all. Greatness is always present in natural human coexistence, when we are not caught up in defending an ideology, a theory, or a political justification. Greatness is present in the nature of collaboration. Greatness is present when we mutually care for one another, when we listen to one another in mutual respect, and when we are open to mutual understanding. Greatness is naturally present, because love is the foundation of human coexistence.

What is rare are the circumstances in which life invites us to act free from ideologies, theories, or political commitments. In these circumstances we unconsciously accept the invitation and act instinctively from love. Most loving acts flow by unnoticed, but sometimes we are fortunate and we witness what should always be visible in human life—namely, that we are naturally loving beings. Ideologies, doctrines, and convictions are the bane of our existence. They trap our intelligence and blind our souls.

The elevated actions demonstrated by the people we have

profiled arise from something that is innate to us—something that is a part of our original nature that we have forgotten. The call of this time is to recover our lost greatness. Whether we believe that we are the children of God, as Dadi Janki does, or that we human beings are loving beings through our biological constitution, as Maturana suggests, the results are the same.

BIBLIOGRAPHY

Buckley, Cara. "A Man Down, a Train Arriving, and a Stranger Makes a Choice." *New York Times*, January 3, 2007, A1.

Carson, Clayborne. *The Autobiography of Martin Luther King, Jr.* New York: Warner Books, 1998, 9 and 28.

Fredrickson, Barbara L. "The Role of Positive Emotions in Positive Psychology: The Broaden-and-Build Theory of Positive Emotions." *American Psychologist* 56 (2001): 218–26.

———. "What Good are Positive Emotions?" *Review of General Psychology* 2, no. 3 (1998): 300–19.

Haidt, Jonathan. "Elevation and the Positive Psychology of Morality." In *Flourishing: Positive Psychology and the Life Well-Lived*, ed. Corey L. M. Keyes and Jonathan Haidt, 275–89. Washington DC: American Psychological Association, 2003.

Montes, Sue Anne Pressley. "In a Moment of Horror, Rousing Acts of Courage." *Washington Post*, January, 13, 2007, Metro section.

CONTRIBUTORS

Hafsat Abiola is a young activist who works to promote women, youth, and democracy in her home country of Nigeria and around the world. She is a founding member of several initiatives, including Global Youth Connect, Youth Employment Campaign, and Vital Voices: Women in Democracy. Abiola is also the founder and president of the Kudirat Initiative for Democracy (KIND), an NGO that seeks to empower democracy and development in Nigeria by strengthening organizations and creating initiatives that advance women. Abiola graduated from Harvard College in 1996 and received an honorary doctorate degree from Haverford College in 2003. She currently lives in China with her husband and two children.

Fr. Pierre Ceyrac is a Jesuit priest who holds a B.A. in classical letters and philology from the Sorbonne, France. He also holds a B.A. in philosophy, theology, Sanskrit, and Tamil. He arrived in India in 1937 and remained there until 1980, when he left to spend thirteen years in a Cambodian refugee camp. He returned to India in 1993 and now lives in Chennai. Fr. Ceyrac's work covers a wide spectrum of activities, which includes emergency and charity work, social work, development work, and recognizing human rights. However, the one area that he talks about with the greatest love is caring for and educating poor and abandoned children.

Barbara Fredrickson is a Kenan distinguished professor of psychology and principal investigator of the Positive Emotions and Psychophysiology Lab at the University of North Carolina. She is a leading scholar within social psychology, affective science, and positive psychology. Her research centers on positive emotions and human flourishing and is supported by grants from the National Institute of Mental Health (NIMH). Her research and teaching have been recognized with numerous honors, including the 2000 American Psychological Association's Templeton Prize in Positive Psychology. Her work is cited widely, and she is regularly invited to give keynote speeches nationally and internationally. She lives in Chapel Hill, North Carolina, with her husband and two sons.

Tex (Louis Willem) Gunning was born in the Netherlands. He holds a degree in economics from Erasmus University, Rotterdam. He is a passionate lecturer, writer, and speaker about the role of business in society and about the need for collective leadership to tackle the world's biggest challenges. Mr. Gunning has been an advisor to many business leaders and academics around the world. His business career has spanned more than twenty-five years in Unilever, ultimately as the business group president of Asia Foods. In September 2007 he was appointed CEO of Vedior, a global company in human research management services. After a successful merger with Randstad, Mr. Gunning joined Akzonobel as the managing director of the decorative paints division.

Jonathan Haidt is an associate professor of psychology at the University of Virginia. He studies the emotional basis of morality and political ideology. He was awarded the Templeton Prize in Positive Psychology in 2001 and the Virginia Outstanding Faculty Award in 2004. He was the Laurance S. Rockefeller distinguished visiting professor at the Princeton University Center for Human Values in 2006–7. Mr. Haidt is the author of *The Happiness Hypothesis: Finding Modern Truth in Ancient Wisdom* (Basic Books, 2006). He is currently writing *The Righteous Mind: Why Good People are Divided by Politics and Religion* (Pantheon, forthcoming).

Dadi Janki is the administrative head of the Brahma Kumaris World Spiritual University (BKWSU). She joined the BKWSU as a founding member in 1937 at the age of twenty-one. After fourteen years of leading a cloistered life of study and yoga, she emerged as a pioneer in translating the life of an ascetic into applied family life. She has also been a leading force in bringing the ancient spiritual wisdom of India to contemporary life beyond India. Dadi Janki is one of the most renowned female spiritual leaders in the world. She serves from two locations: Mount Abu, India, the world headquarters of the Brahma Kumaris; and London, England, the international coordinating office of the Brahma Kumaris. Although she is ninety-three at the time of the publication of this book, her feeling that the world needs spiritual power at this time inspires her to maintain a rigorous lecture and worldwide touring schedule.

Dr. Abdul Kalam was the eleventh president of India from 2002 to 2007. He is an aeronautical engineer and is renowned for his role in developing India's defense research. Dr. Kalam is also a prolific author and a source of inspiration to the people of India. He says, "I personally believe when the nation is progressing toward economic development, it is also essential to build education with a value system drawn from our civilization heritage. The good human life comes out of the way we live. We may have series of problems, but the billion people have the connectivity which gives us the united strength."

Humberto Maturana (Romesín) is a biologist. He has worked for many years on the biology of cognition at the University of Chile in Santiago, Chile. Since 2000, he has dedicated all of his time to the Matriztic Institute, where he and Ximena Dávila Yáñez have developed and expanded the understanding of the Biologico-Cultural Matrix of Human Existence as a new vision of the fundamental biologico-cultural nature of humanness. He lives in Santiago with his wife, Beatriz.

Federico Mayor (Zaragoza) is a biochemist by profession, but his passion is peace. He served as director general of UNESCO (United Nations Educational, Scientific, and Cultural Organization) from 1987–99. During his tenure with UNESCO, Dr. Mayor highlighted universal core values as fundamental in the promotion of multilateral solutions to global problems. His leadership in the International Year of Tolerance and the International Year of Peace and Non-Violence led to a decade of peace and nonviolence for the children of the world. He presently chairs Fundación Cultura de Paz (Foundation for the Culture of Peace), which he founded in 2000 and operates out of Madrid, Spain.

Bart McGettrick is an emeritus professor of education at the University of Glasgow. He is also a professor of educational development and the deputy dean of education at Liverpool Hope University. He was the first dean of the faculty of education at the University of Glasgow. His work in education and public life started when he was a teacher. In 1985 he was appointed principal of St. Andrew's College in Scotland. His growing interest in the development of education and his own personal interest in global inclusivity have taken him to every continent except Antarctica.

Dr. Zilda Arns Neumann is a pediatrician who founded and leads Pastoral da Criança (the Pastoral of the Child), an innovative public health program that works with more than 265,000 volunteers to help poor families in her native Brazil. "Children are the seed for peace or violence in the future, depending on how they are cared for and stimulated," she says of her work. "Thus, their family and community environment must be sown to grow a fairer and more fraternal world, a world to serve life and hope." Nominated for the Nobel Peace Prize in 2005, Neumann has received numerous other honors for her work.

Brooke Rodgers has a B.F.A. in general sculptural studies from Maryland Institute College of Art. She has a B.S. from State University of New York (SUNY) at Stonybrook in New York and is currently a graduate student in marine science at the same university.

PERMISSIONS

111

ACKNOWLEDGMENTS

The writing of this book was in truth a pilgrimage, and we simply could not have done it without the extraordinary guidance and support we received every step of the way. Of course, the pilgrimage was inspired by the life and love of Dadi Janki, who, once she consented to allow the book to be written, made herself available for many interviews in which she explained the deep spiritual principles behind our questions.

We offer our humble and limitless gratitude and appreciation to Humberto Maturana, who was generous beyond anything we could ever have requested. He made himself available for many days in Chile for mutual reflection and then stayed with us every step of the way through draft after draft of the manuscript, guiding us back again and again to simple and profound truth.

Tex Gunning, for whom an understanding of applied greatness is a lifelong interest, encouraged and inspired us when we began to flag, and generously supported us in our search. Of course, there were all of those who consented to be interviewed: Hafsat Abiola, Father Pierre Ceyrac, Abdul Kalam, Bart McGettrick, Federico Mayor Zaragoza, Zilda Arns Neumann, and Brooke Rodgers. Each was patient, thoughtful, and generous. We are grateful too for those who facilitated these interviews—Sister Asha and Brother Brij Mohan in India, Christina Carvalho Pinto in Brazil, Angelica Fanjul in Chile, Sister Jayanti Kirpalani in England, Father Dominque Peccoud in France, Rita Cleary in the United States, and Miriam Subirana in Spain.

At certain critical points we benefited greatly by the thinking partnership of Peter Senge and Sister Mohini Panjabi. We are also grateful to Jean Brennan for the cover design.

INDEX

ABOUT THE AUTHORS

Judy Rodgers has spent her life working at the intersection of media, education, and business. She received a B.A. from the University of Michigan and an M.A. in English from Miami University in Oxford, Ohio. For the next twenty years, she worked as a professor of English, a writer in radio, a producer in video, and as an entrepreneur of media projects to educate leaders in business. She worked with thought leaders such as Walter Cronkite and best selling authors such as John Naisbitt, Tom Peters, and Peter Senge.

She is interested in the ways that important ideas reach

the broadest possible audience. This has led her to launch media projects and to start businesses, foundations, centers, and initiatives to support the movement of important ideas. In 1985 she joined three other investors in a leveraged buyout of a division of CBS-Fox Video, which became Video Publishing House, an educational video publishing company in Chicago, specializing in cutting edge theories of management, leadership, and change.

In the early to mid1990's she met people and encountered new theory and knowledge that transformed her life and work. She studied the Ontology of Language, through which she first encountered cognitive biologist Humberto Maturana. She studied the emerging field of positive psychology and the theory and practice of Appreciative Inquiry with David Cooperrider. And she began to study raja yoga with the Brahma Kumaris (bkwsu.org.). This marked a shift in her focus: she began to consider the relationship between awareness, thought, ways of seeing, language, and action.

In 1997 she founded the Communication Architecture Group, through which she manages communications and media projects, organizational consulting, and coaching. In 1999 she co-founded a global conversation initiative with the media called Images and Voices of Hope to strengthen the role of media as a constructive force in society. She continues as director of Images and Voices of Hope (ivofhope.org).

In 2003 she co-founded, with Management Professor David Cooperrider, the Center for Business as an Agent of World Benefit at the Weatherhead School of Management at Case Western Reserve University.

Something Beyond Greatness: Conversations with a Man of Science and a Woman of God is a continuation of her inquiry into the relationship between inner awareness, thought, seeing, and action.

Gayatri Naraine has been the Brahma Kumaris' (BK's) representative to the United Nations since 1980. When she first met the BKs as a young woman in 1975, she was working at the University of Guyana in the office of the Dean of Education. In 1978, she came to the United States, and soon after her arrival began to facilitate the Brahma Kumaris' representation with the United Nations in New York, beginning with the Department of Public Information (DPI). She was successful in obtaining formal affiliation to DPI for the Brahma Kumaris in 1980. After three years she was convinced that spirituality and values were a necessary yet missing ingredient in the work of the UN, and she began working to secure a consultative status for the Brahma Kumaris in the Economic and Social